SOCIAL CHANGE AND SOCIAL ISSUES IN THE FORMER USSR

SELECTED PAPERS FROM THE FOURTH WORLD
CONGRESS FOR SOVIET AND EAST EUROPEAN
STUDIES, HARROGATE, 1990

*Edited for the International Council for Soviet and East European Studies by Stephen
White, Professor of Politics, University of Glasgow*

From the same publishers:

Roy Allison (*editor*)
RADICAL REFORM IN SOVIET DEFENCE POLICY

Ben Eklof (*editor*)
SCHOOL AND SOCIETY IN TSARIST AND SOVIET RUSSIA

John Elsworth (*editor*)
THE SILVER AGE IN RUSSIAN LITERATURE

John Garrard and Carol Garrard (*editors*)
WORLD WAR 2 AND THE SOVIET PEOPLE

Zvi Gitelman (*editor*)
THE POLITICS OF NATIONALITY AND THE EROSION OF THE USSR

Sheelagh Duffin Graham (*editor*)
NEW DIRECTIONS IN SOVIET LITERATURE

Celia Hawkesworth (*editor*)
LITERATURE AND POLITICS IN EASTERN EUROPE

Lindsey Hughes (*editor*)
NEW PERSPECTIVES ON MUSCOVITE HISTORY

Walter Joyce (*editor*)
SOCIAL CHANGE AND SOCIAL ISSUES IN THE FORMER USSR

Bohdan Krawchenko (*editor*)
UKRAINIAN PAST, UKRAINIAN PRESENT

Paul G. Lewis (*editor*)
DEMOCRACY AND CIVIL SOCIETY IN EASTERN EUROPE

Robert B. McKean (*editor*)
NEW PERSPECTIVES IN MODERN RUSSIAN HISTORY

John Morison (*editor*)
THE CZECH AND SLOVAK EXPERIENCE
EASTERN EUROPE AND THE WEST

John O. Norman (*editor*)
NEW PERSPECTIVES ON RUSSIAN AND SOVIET ARTISTIC CULTURE

Derek Offord (*editor*)
THE GOLDEN AGE OF RUSSIAN LITERATURE AND THOUGHT

Michael E. Urban (*editor*)
IDEOLOGY AND SYSTEM CHANGE IN THE USSR AND EAST EUROPE

Social Change and Social Issues in the Former USSR

**Selected Papers from the Fourth World Congress
for Soviet and East European Studies, Harrogate, 1990**

Edited by

Walter Joyce
Research Fellow
Institute of Soviet and East European Studies
University of Glasgow

St. Martin's Press

First published in Great Britain 1992 by
THE MACMILLAN PRESS LTD
Houndmills, Basingstoke, Hampshire RG21 2XS
and London
Companies and representatives
throughout the world

This book is published in association with the International Council
for Soviet and East European Studies

A catalogue record for this book is available
from the British Library.

ISBN 0–333–55328–4

Printed in Great Britain by
Billing and Sons Ltd
Worcester

First published in the United States of America 1992 by
Scholarly and Reference Division,
ST. MARTIN'S PRESS, INC.,
175 Fifth Avenue,
New York, N.Y. 10010

ISBN 0–312–07994–X

Library of Congress Cataloging-in-Publication Data
World Congress for Soviet and East European Studies (4th : 1990 :
Harrogate, England)
Social change and social issues in the former USSR :
selected papers from the Fourth World Congress for Soviet and East
European Studies, Harrogate, 1990 / edited by Walter Joyce.
p. cm.
includes index.
ISBN 0–312–07994–X
1. Soviet Union—Social conditions—1970-   —Congresses.
I. Walter Joyce, 1936–   .   II. International Council for Soviet
and East European Studies.   III. Title.
HN523.5.W67   1992
306'.0947—dc20   92–3479
                                                            CIP

Contents

General Editor's Introduction

The Fourth World Congress for Soviet and East European Studies took place in Harrogate, Yorkshire, in July 1990. It was an unusual congress in many ways. It was the first of its kind to take place in Britain, and the first to take place since the launching of Gorbachev's programme of *perestroika* and the revolutions in Eastern Europe (indeed so rapid was the pace of change in the countries with which we were concerned that the final programme had to incorporate over 600 amendments). It was the largest and most complex congress of Soviet and East European studies that has yet taken place, with twenty-seven panels spread over fourteen sessions on six days. It was also the most representative congress of its kind, with over two thousand participants including – for the first time – about three hundred from the USSR and Eastern Europe. Most were scholars, some were activists, and a few were the new kind of academic turned part-time deputy: whatever their status, it was probably this Soviet and East European presence that contributed most directly to making this a very different congress from the ones that had preceded it in the 1970s and 1980s.

No series of volumes, however numerous, could hope to convey the full flavour of this extraordinary occasion. The formal panels alone incorporated almost a thousand papers. There were three further plenary sessions; there were many more unattached papers; and the subjects that were treated ranged from medieval Novgorod to computational linguistics, from the problems of the handicapped in the USSR to Serbian art at the time of the battle of Kosovo. Nor, it was decided at an early stage, would it even be desirable to attempt a fully comprehensive 'congress proceedings', including all the papers in their original form. My aim as General Editor, with the strong support of the International Council for Soviet and East European Studies (who co-sponsored the congress with the British Association for Soviet, Slavonic and East European Studies), has rather been to generate a series of volumes which will have some thematic coherence, and to bring them out as quickly as possible while their (often topical) contents are still current.

A strategy of this kind imposes a cost, in that many authors have had to find other outlets for what would in different circumstances have been very publishable papers. The gain, however, seems much greater: a series of real books on properly defined subjects, edited by scholars of experience and standing in their respective fields, and placed promptly before the academic community. These, I am glad to say, were the same as the objectives of the publishers that expressed an interest in various aspects of the congress proceedings, and it has led to a series of volumes as well as of special issues of journals covering a wide range of interests.

There are volumes on art and architecture, on history and literature, on law and economics, on society and education. There are further volumes on nationality issues and the Ukraine, on the environment, on international relations and on defence. There are Soviet volumes, and others that deal more specifically with Eastern (or perhaps more properly, East Central) Europe. There are inter-disciplinary volumes on women in Russia and the USSR, the Soviet experience in World War II, and ideology and system change. There are special issues of some of the journals that publish in our field, dealing with religion and Slovene studies, émigrés and East European economics, publishing and politics, linguistics and the Russian revolution. Altogether nearly forty separate publications will stem from the Harrogate congress: more than twice as many as from any previous congress of its kind, and a rich and enduring record of its deliberations.

Most of these volumes will be published in the United Kingdom by Macmillan, and in the United States by St Martin's Press. It is my pleasant duty to acknowledge Macmillan's early interest in the scho-larly output of the congress, and the swift and professional attention that has been given to all of these volumes since their inception. A full list of the Macmillan Harrogate series appears elsewhere in the Macmillan edition of this volume; it can give only an impression of the commitment and support I have enjoyed from Tim Farmiloe, Clare Wace and others at all stages of our proceedings. I should also take this opportunity to thank John Morison and his colleagues on the International Council for Soviet and East European Studies for entrusting me with this responsible task in the first place, and the various sponsors – the Erasmus Prize Fund of Amsterdam, the Ford Foundation in New York, the British Foreign and Commonwealth Office, the British Council, the Stefan Batory Trust and others – whose generous support helped to make the congress a reality.

The next congress will be held in 1995, and (it is hoped) at a location in Eastern Europe. Its proceedings can hardly hope to improve upon the vigour and imagination that is so abundantly displayed on the pages of these splendid volumes.

University of Glasgow STEPHEN WHITE

Preface

This book is made up of a selection of the many papers that were delivered at the Fourth World Congress for Soviet and East European Studies in Harrogate, 21–26 July 1990, on the more intractable problems of Soviet society. The advent of the Gorbachev era has meant not only access to previously unpublished information but also a greater readiness to measure the achievements and failures of Soviet society against those of the non-communist world without resort to ideological sophistry. Nonetheless, the papers that are included in this volume testify to the persistence of the belief that social order and well-being are imperatives in a socialist society and, as such, that they are largely achievable by government decree.

Thus Gregory Andrusz, in the opening contribution to the volume, analyses the failure of the state monopoly of housing construction and allocation to satisfy the demand for housing, with the more vulnerable sections of Soviet society – pensioners, veterans and others – suffering particularly badly. Indeed, the drift is now to a regulated market in housing with the state acting merely as 'facilitator'. Andrusz argues that such a regulated market might well, paradoxically, allow housing to be allocated on a more egalitarian basis.

The official sanctioning of private cooperatives, notes Lars Ohlsson, led immediately to clashes between them and the command economy and administration. Unsurprisingly, too, while it was assumed that the new cooperatives would rush to join the market, the fact is that conditions of arbitrary regulation of supply and administrative harassment have seen the bulk of co-operative activity orientated to state enterprises and geared to satisfying the system of state orders. The position of the co-operatives has also not been helped by popular accusations of profiteering and corruption. Attempts to regulate any such excesses have, in their turn, merely led to the reimposition of the command-administrative system. However, concludes Ohlsson, even in such unpromising circumstances there has been very considerable growth in the co-operative movement, and recruits to the new system emphasise the greater freedom of action and release from state regulation.

John Kramer, in his paper, notes the failure, before the new openness, even to acknowledge the existence of the drug abuse problem. In such circumstances, not only is the researcher faced with the difficulties of incomplete data, but abusers are not well informed of the consequences of their abuse. This inadequacy of response also characterises state anti-drug abuse initiatives, which are often sub-sumed under institutions concerned primarily with alcoholism and mental health. Legal sanctions, too, are held to be too lenient to deter successfully. The dilemma, then, is to decide whether abuse is a legal or a medical problem. The previous Soviet tradition of depicting drug abuse as an example of Western decadence has given way to the acceptance of such phenomena as the common experience of all societies, and to a new readiness to look carefully at international experience and treatment methods.

One of the main general conclusions of Blum's paper on regional diversity in the main trends of Soviet mortality is that 'traditional' patterns have retained a remarkable continuity. As with the other papers, statistical analysis shows up the deadening effect of rigid centralization. Unfortunately, any exercise of this kind is hampered by the lack of complete data, especially on infant mortality. In the paper the mortality patterns of the Western Soviet republics are compared with those of other European countries, while those of the Central Asian republics are compared with the mortality patterns of developing countries. Blum argues that while a strictly planned (and ill-adapted) policy can easily lead to a decrease in the most prominent and evident causes of death, such a situation is ever fragile and very likely over the long run to lead to deterioration.

A complementary demographic study of sex differentials in Soviet mortality by Kingkade and Arriaga emphasises the excess male over female mortality. The authors point out, for example, that the anti-alcoholism drive was a typical short-term response to negative lifestyle factors. While noting certain favourable trends in Soviet mortality statistics since 1985, the authors emphasise that the sex differential in favour of women in the USSR remains one of the largest in the world. In common with the other authors of this collection Kingkade and Arriaga point out the continuing inad-equacies of a system still having difficulty adapting, but they also see hope in new and more eclectic approaches to problems.

The anti-alcohol campaign launched in May 1985 was intended as an all-out attempt to eradicate an age-old (especially Russian) scourge by a combination of increasingly harsh legislation, re-direction of the drink-related part of the economy, and a concerted campaign of moral and social admonition. As we see from the other papers, the fundamental assumption was that any and every social problem in a socialist society was amenable to solutions from above, an assumption anywhere and everywhere found in practice to be wrong. Walter Joyce's paper on this now-abandoned grand design briefly compares it with previous anti-alcohol campaigns, and then attempts to evaluate the armoury of legislative and other sanctions which the state had at its disposal. The conclusion is that the late realisation of the impossibility of a speedy social change of this kind, together with the economic arguments against complete abstinence, helped to facilitate the emergence of more enlightened approaches on the part of the society itself.

The final paper in the collection treats of the impact on the veterans of an unpopular and ultimately unwinnable war in Afghanistan, and of the veterans on a society ill-equipped and even ill-disposed either to reward or to compensate them. Instead of 'homes fit for heroes', the 'Afgantsy' have been given little help towards resettlement. The prostheses which have been supplied to the disabled are in the main of very poor quality, and the psychologically damaged are left to find solace in drink or drugs. Jim Riordan draws attention in the paper to the potentially destabilising effects on Soviet (and now post-Soviet) society of such pockets of grievance. On the other hand, the readiness of many veterans to organise to secure their due place in society is very much in tune with a period when the future of that society is, as never before, subject to deep debate.

WALTER JOYCE

Notes on the Contributors

Gregory Andrusz is Senior Lecturer in Sociology at Middlesex Polytechnic, Enfield, UK. He is the author of articles on Soviet housing, local government and co-operatives, and is currently completing a project on the co-operative movement in the Soviet Union and Europe with special reference to housing.

Alain Blum is Head of Research at the Institut National d'Etudes Démographiques in Paris, where he specialises in demographic studies of the Soviet Union. He has written a number of studies on long- and short-interaction between political structure, ideological change and social behaviour.

Walter Joyce is Research Fellow in the Institute of Soviet and East European Studies, University of Glasgow, Scotland. The joint author of *Gorbachev and Gorbachevism* (1989), he has written articles on Soviet regional economic development and is currently engaged on a project on the Baltic republics.

W. Ward Kingkade and **Eduardo E. Arriaga** are members of the US Bureau of the Census, Washington, DC. Both authors have written widely on aspects of Soviet demography.

John M. Kramer is Distinguished Professor of Political Science, Mary Washington College, Virginia, USA. His most recent publication is *The Energy Gap in Eastern Europe* (1990).

Lars Ohlsson is Reader in the Department of Soviet and East European Studies, Uppsala University, Sweden. He is the author of a study of local government in the Soviet Union, and has written articles on the process of *perestroika*.

Jim Riordan is Head of Linguistics and International Studies and Professor of Russian Studies, University of Surrey, UK. He has written books on Soviet sport and youth culture; his most recent publication (with Sue Bridger) is *Dear Comrade Editor* (1992).

1 The Market as Distributor of Housing under Socialism: its Virtues and Vices

Gregory Andrusz

Although this chapter is concerned with housing policy, three points should be made at the outset to indicate the cultural pitfalls that arise when interpretations of events and social phenomena are too reliant on simple dictionary translations.

First of all, Western governments and their publics were keen to see the USSR begin to transform itself from an administrative-command into a market-based economy. The two types of system are simplified into 'plan' and 'market'. Party conferences, speeches by leading political functionaries and articles and letters to the press by professional economists and members of the public frequently refer to some aspect or other of the 'market'.

The word in Russian for 'market' is *rynok*. However, the Western concept of 'market' has profound, culturally-hegemonic meanings. When Nikolai Petrakov, a corresponding member of the USSR Academy of Sciences and presidential adviser on economic affairs, states that 'the market existed thousands of years ago', he reveals a fundamental misunderstanding of the significance and use of the concept in the West.[1] It seems to me that in cultural terms, in the minds of the majority of the Soviet population, the opposite to the planned, administrative command economy is not a *rynok* but a *yarmarka*, which is a market in the sense of a fair.

Secondly, the Russian language has contributed few words to the international lexicon. *Bystro* is one of the better known ones. (The Russians used the term *bystro* when in Paris following the defeat of Napoleon. Hence bistro [quickly] was the first fast food restaurant!) Fewer use the term *lishnyi chelovek* (superfluous person). Mr Gorbachev's lasting achievement will undoubtedly be his introduction into the global vocabulary of the word *perestroika*. The reasons for the widespread acceptance of this term are various. One of them is

1

that 'restructuring' has a totally different connotation from 'revolution', a term that Gorbachev has said is synonymous with 'perestroika'. The word 'revolution' is normally associated with left-wing movements; 'restructuring', whether used by Gorbachev or Mrs Thatcher, leans towards what is conventionally designated 'the right'. The restructuring of British industry and economy, like that in the Soviet Union, has meant a turn away from the state and planning to private enterprise and market forces.

Thirdly, different stages in the emergence of a housing policy may be identified. The Party Programme lays down very general goals for housing policy while the Constitution includes a clause on the right of Soviet citizens to accommodation. Resolutions passed at Party Congresses indicate, still in general terms, the broad strategy to be applied to reach the aims laid down in the Constitution and Programme. These become formulated in general decrees. Yet one of the eternal problems with Soviet 'legislation' is the status of different types of governmental order. One of the most common types is the decree (*postanovlenie*). It varies in length, from less than a page to forty pages. Except for those which alter specific clauses in earlier decrees or nullify them altogether, they are purposely couched in vague terms. This has the advantage of enabling them to be modified quickly in the light of experience and changing needs.

However, lacking the status of law, the organisation at which this decree is directed finds it too easy to ignore it. This has been the fate of the majority of decrees on housing; clearly visible is the singular lack of success of housing co-operatives since the first post-war decree encouraging their formation in 1962.

So, even decrees which are issued by the Central Committee of the CPSU and the USSR Council of Ministers, and signed by the General Secretary, are not binding. In so far as they are not laws (*zakon*), they often appear to represent little other than declarations of intent. This should be borne in mind in the discussion which follows.

THE CONTEXT

1. Housing Objectives and the Contemporary Situation

The XXVII Congress passed a resolution to provide each family with its own separate flat or house by the year 2000. In order to do so, 40 million new flats and individual houses (2.1–2.3 billion square metres of overall space) will have to be erected in the 15 year period, 1986–2000, which will mean doubling the existing housing stock. A major report produced by the country's foremost research institute in 1988 proposes three variants of the basic goal, based on an estimated population in the year 2000 of 313.4 million people, composed of 98 million households. The first is to build 2.25 billion square metres (giving 17.8 square metres per person); the second, 2.8, and the third, 3.1 billion square metres.[2] It concluded that the second variant should be adopted as the minimum to be achieved.[3] This would provide by the year 2000 an average of 19.5 square metres of overall living space per person, compared with 15.5 square metres at the beginning of 1989.

In actual fact, in the four years, 1986–89, housing construction was on average 16 per cent higher than during the 11th five year plan period, and it is anticipated that by the end of 1990, 650 million square metres of housing space will have been erected during the current 12th five year plan. This will be 100 million square metres more than in the previous five year plan, even though the target for 1989 was not achieved because of the shortage of building materials and delivery delays. Despite this overall quantitative success, the housing situation remains 'acute' (*ostrii*): over six million families are still living in communal flats or hostels, or are in privately rented accommodation. This includes 4.7 per cent of families and single persons living in shared accommodation and 12 million people (4.2 per cent of the total population) living in hostels. Over 14 million people are on the waiting list to improve their housing conditions. One-third of the population (100–120 million people) still live below the 'sanitary norm' of 9 square metres (which, according to the deputy chairman of Gosstroi, it is the 'state's sacred duty to provide free of charge').[4] Despite the rate of construction, this list is not diminishing. Yet even some of these figures on the magnitude of the problem are contested, largely because of different interpretations of the word 'family'. A further 4.5 million families have less than 5 square metres per person, but for some reason they are not on waiting lists.[5] In order to remedy this situation, the rate of house building has to increase to 900 million square metres during the 13th five year plan (1991–5) and over 1 billion in 1996–2000. This would improve the living conditions of a further 110–120 million people.

According to Kolotilikin, a well-known and respected housing specialist, planners omit to consider in need of housing, individuals in the 20–30 age range, since they already have homes with their families. As a result of leaving out this population group, planners seriously underestimate the need for housing. There is too little detailed (and consistent) data to assess the validity of his challenge, but his calculations of need certainly deserve attention.

He concludes that by the year 2000 the country will have 119 million households in contrast to Gosplan's estimate of 97 million. So, instead of the projected 36 million new homes which are to be provided in the period 1986–2000, the figure should be 54 million. (In both estimates, 16 million units will be needed to replace urban and rural dwellings demolished because of their dilapidation.) In all likelihood, he contends, by the turn of the century, some people will still be sharing flats [*kommunal'naya kvartira*]; extended families will continue to be obliged to live together; a large number of single persons and families will be in hostels (where the former will share a room); and there will be a lack of institutional care for orphans, senior citizens and the disabled and handicapped.

The balance of evidence – based essentially on a knowledge of current living conditions of a large number of families, reasonable demographic projections and changing (subjective) needs and demands – does lend support to Kolotilkin's estimates. Some of his findings and fears are acknowledged in that 'in many parts of the country, housing construction cannot keep pace with family formation'.[6]

2. The Ownership of Soviet Housing

Soviet housing policy was established under the exigencies of revolution and civil war. Two new tenures were created, the municipalised and nationalised, the former being owned and operated by the local soviets and the latter by economic agencies and public bodies. The introduction of the New Economic Policy (NEP) in 1921 witnessed changes in housing policy. The state divested itself of the responsibility for small houses. When new building began again in 1923 it was the private sector which took the initiative and was counted upon to meet demand. Legislation passed as late as 1928 anticipated attracting both the savings of individual workers into building houses for themselves and the larger resources of private entrepreneurs for building to rent. De-municipalisation was integral to this policy. In its search for ways to finance house building in 1924 the government introduced another quasi-private form of tenure, the housing co-operative.[7] This was more important theoretically and ideologically than in terms of its practical impact on the housing shortage. Its abolition in 1937, restitution during the Khrushchevian thaw in 1962, and the strong sponsorship which it has received from Gorbachev suggest that, in the history of Soviet housing and domestic policy generally, the co-operative sector has served as a reliable barometer of change in Soviet society.

In 1990 the four tenure categories which had emerged by 1924 continued to be the pillars of house ownership: (1) local soviet (the former 'municipalised' sector); (2) state ministries, enterprises, trade unions (formerly, the 'nationalised' sector, and now named the 'departmental' stock); (3) housing co-operatives; (4) individual home ownership. The essential distinction between categories 1 and 2 (the state sector) is that while the task of the former is to allocate housing to individuals living within their administrative jurisdiction, the departmental sector provides accommodation for those with whom it has a 'productive relationship'.

3. Recent Legislation

Three important housing decrees were published in February, March and December 1988 and all marked, in the consistency of their prime objectives, a major change in policy direction. In some ways they bear a resemblance to housing policy goals adopted during NEP.

The first of them came in the decree of February 1988 entitled 'On Measures to Accelerate the Development of Individual Housing Construction'. At the beginning of the year it represented the most radical of all post-war government promulgations on housing policy.[8] 'This type of construction', it pointed out, 'relying on the labour of the population and more fully using its increased spending power derived from higher incomes and from money held in savings banks, is becoming one of the most important ways of activating the human factor'. Of course, savings deposits are an obvious target for the government and in a period of open inflation and economic insecurity it also makes sense for citizens to invest in property.

The contribution expected to be made by the owner-occupied sector is to increase quite considerably. In comparison with 1985, when it erected 16.3 million square metres of living space (14.4 per cent of all housing construction), by 1995 this sector should have erected 60 million square metres, and 200 million during the course of the 13th five year plan. By the end of the century, 'housing erected by the population' will comprise on aggregate 29.3 per cent of all accommodation built and 19.7 per cent of that erected in urban areas, compared with 17.1 and 8.8 per cent respectively in 1988. The new 'legislation' thus signals a reversal of the long-term decline of this 'private sector' over a 30-year period.

This reversal is to be brought about by a combination of initiatives: (i) banks are to make credit available to enterprises intending to start or expand production of building and decorating materials; (ii) preference in the allocation of building plots should be given to people surrendering their public sector accommodation to the local soviet; (iii) the areas set aside for individual housing development must be provided with access roads and all public utilities; (iv) state banks are to be allowed to make advances of up to 20 000 roubles repayable over 25 years in towns and 50 years in the countryside. This increases the size of the loan from 3000 roubles and extends the repayment period from 10 years. The same favourable terms are to be granted to people wishing to purchase individual homes, an important requirement for the further-ance of an open housing market. The development of a housing market will be enhanced by allowing enterprises and organisations to sell houses to their workers, if the latter pay them 'no less' than 40 per cent of the value of the house over a period of 50 years in the countryside. The corresponding figures for urban dwellers are 50 per cent and 25 years. This was the nearest the Soviet Union has ever come to the UK policy of selling council housing.

In so far as 'encouraging the population to use its resources' to expand the supply of housing has in recent years been directed at least as much to the house-building co-operative as the owner-occupied sector, it was to be expected that the increased benefits accruing to the latter would soon be accompanied by amendments to legislation governing co-operatives. This duly occurred in March 1988 in the decree 'On Measures to Accelerate the Development of Hous-ing Co-operatives'.[9] The preamble of complaints on the lack of success of this form of tenure to date was followed by the statement that housing co-operatives would become 'one of the main ways for expanding housing construction . . . so that by 1995 they will contri-bute no less than two to three times more than at present to the overall volume of housing construction'. According to the housing researchers attached to TsNIIEP zhilishche, using the government's 1987 projections, by 1996–2000 co-operatives will account for 30 per cent of new building in towns. (This represents 97 per cent of all co-operative construction and thus confirms the urban nature of this form of tenure.) In 1988 they erected 9.5 per cent of all housing in towns.

The legislation defines two types of co-operative. The first consists of house-building co-operatives specifically created for the purpose of constructing and running dwellings by and for the benefit of the membership. They are allowed to acquire buildings in need of major capital repairs, renovate them and then occupy them. The second type of co-operative is not concerned with building at all; it is set up in order to acquire existing housing, either newly erected or reno-vated, from enterprises and the local soviets. These properties are being offered at a huge discount, since the purchaser has to pay 'not less than 20–25 per cent of the property's assessed value', with the balance to be paid off over 25 years. As an incentive to local soviets to cease acting obstructively towards the co-operatives, those soviets are allowed to add a supplement of up to 15 per cent of the cost of construction in those cases where co-operatives are located 'in the most favourable neighbourhoods'. The supplementary charge is to be paid into the local budget. This policy innovation has a twofold significance. First, it tends to increase the budgetary autonomy of local soviets. Second, the payment represents a differential rent and therefore a step towards making the charge for accommodation reflect location, which has long been advocated.[10] The creation of co-operatives to purchase older and newly erected buildings from the state was symptomatic of the shift towards acceptance of the principle that at least part of the state housing stock may legitimately be privatised.

In December 1988 the logic of these developments culminated in the Politbureau's acceptance of proposals made by the Council of Ministers to allow local soviets and enterprises to transfer dwellings controlled by them into private ownership. It allows sitting tenants to buy their flats subject to reconstruction and major capital repair.[11] At present the local soviets have been given considerable discretion in deciding on their sales policy and setting the rules for service and maintenance charges for individuals who want to buy their flats.

A principal position of senior Central Committee members active in the field of housing policy is that the key objective, of furnishing each family with its own home, will only be achievable by first of all creating and securing an environment for, and then guaranteeing the existence of, different forms of housing tenure. This declaration is often accompanied by the parenthetic remark that these different types of tenure 'correspond to the needs of different social groups'.

Ideas differ on which social groups should have access to which type of tenure. However, one authoritative view (that of Stashenkov) makes the following prescription: (1) those being offered accommodation in new housing erected using central government funds should be employees in state factories and agricultural enterprises and members of the armed forces; (2) housing built by local soviets should be reserved for those whose living conditions are substandard and for pensioners, invalids and employees in the service sector, such as doctors and teachers; (3) dwellings erected by enterprise and organisations using their own funds should be reserved for members of these work collectives.[12]

4. Societal Crisis and Change

Changes in housing policy are contained within the framework of the democratisation of the political system and privatisation in the economy. These two processes involve sharpening political conflicts between polarised political ideologies and also major reforms to the monetary system and the creation of wholly new financial institutions, such as private banks and insurance. It is almost universally accepted that monetary reform and attendant price restrictions and policies to deal with adverse balance of payments and inflation will inevitably bring unemployment. At the heart of these changes is the creation of different forms of property ownership. This has a direct effect on housing, both its production and distribution. (It hardly needs stating that the crises which are being witnessed extend well beyond the bounds of managing the economy.)[13]

An examination of the changing policy towards housing in the Soviet Union requires it to be located within the *institutional* framework of the past – a past which, under Soviet conditions, is very often the present. *Perestroika* was initially concerned with the restructuring of the economic system. Its appeal to the 'cadres' was first couched in terms of 'efficiency'. When the seriousness of the economic situation became more evident, 'perestroika' came to be regarded as the sole means for ensuring system survival.

Because of the reluctance of various social groups between 1986 and 1988 to recognise the severity of the malaise, and their even greater reluctance to contemplate 'deep' restructuring, Mr Gorbachev inaugurated *glasnost'*. Additionally, since people do not live by bread alone – that is, 'efficiency' is an insufficient motivator – he reactivated the moral appeal of 'social justice'. In doing so he allowed journalists to open the gate to the Aladdin's cave of party privilege. Gorbachev encouraged them to reveal the injustices of privilege to their readerships and audiences. Some of them – Starkov, the editor of *Argumenty i fakty*, for example – were thought by Gorbachev to have gone too far. Their revelations, together with the sometimes exaggerated claims of publicists and the manipulative falsifications of demagogues, were supplemented, modified, corrected and interpreted by social scientists, particularly sociologists. The task of the latter is now to understand society and to develop theories to interpret its social structure and stratification system, instead of perpetuating myths about the Soviet Union being a 'classless' society whose nations are being drawn closer together.

5. Soviet Housing Serfs

An understanding of the housing situation in the Soviet Union has to begin by examining the importance of the social functions performed by enterprises for their workforce and the relationship of enterprises to local authorities (local soviets).

With the removal of industry from the control of urban soviets as early as 1918, the latter lost their economic base. By the 1920s they were impecunious and as a consequence lacked power. With the revival of industry and the onset of rapid industrialisation, the state's attention was concentrated upon manufacturing industry, and investment funds were concentrated in the hands of the major industrial ministries, who were then charged with providing for the needs of the labour forces which they employed. During the 1930s industrial enterprises came to control virtually all the funds allocated for providing the social infrastructure in the cities where they were sited. The use of consumer goods and services, including housing, provided by factories was restricted to the factory's own employees and closed to the rest of the city's inhabitants.

In today's system large enterprises – those which supply a national market – are controlled by All-Union ministries from the centre, from whom they receive their orders and resources. The revenue generated by these enterprises is ploughed back into the state budget and then redistributed according to the Government's priorities. (For instance, the car assembly plant, AZLK, responsible for producing the 'Moskvich', pays only 2.3 per cent of its turnover tax into the Moscow city budget.)

The incomes of the local soviets have never been sufficient for them to provide an adequate social infrastructure. This has made it necessary for the 'city fathers' to go cap in hand to the large enterprises for financial support. The latter have frequently responded by expanding their social activities in order to provide for their workforce, to the extent that some even become totally independent from the city's service structure. The outcome of this situation is that when choosing an occupation or firm, the worker is more attracted by the social benefits to be gained than from the work itself or even the salary. The 'richer' factory or enterprise is better placed to attract better workers. Concomitantly, those unable to offer such a range of services (including food products) are unable to compete and often suffer from labour shortages. Many of the very largest enterprises, especially those having their 'own neighbourhoods', operate like paternalistic corporations, even organising lectures and concerts and large sporting events.

This system leads to enormous anomalies. Huge housing estates, almost totally lacking in basic health services and leisure facilities, can lie next to factories which have enormous palaces of culture and other amenities that are frequently empty or only partly used. Because they are closed to outsiders, they suffer from underuse (canteens open for only a few hours a day) while the city's open social infrastructure is grossly overloaded. The outcome is that cities become divided into zones, often definable in terms of the factory to which they belong and by the whole quality of their environments, including their social-psychological climate. Thus, while it is difficult to identify poor or ethnic districts in cities, neighbourhood boundaries are observable in terms of whether they 'belong' to a rich or poor factory. In the case of the former, buildings will be modern and well painted and there will be a range of shops, social facilities and kindergartens, whereas the latter will be surrounded by dilapidated housing.

The actual sums allocated for housing, and the infrastructure more generally, depend on the industrial branch to which the enterprise belongs and, of course, its size. The larger and more successful it is, the larger its profit and thus the resources that it has to dispense. So, for example, the size of the social fund of a worker in the chemical industry is 40 times greater than someone working in the food-processing industry. In 1982 the Energy & Electricity sector erected 2.49 square metres per employee, compared with 0.22 and 0.19 square metres by the Light Industry and Food Processing sectors respectively.[14] But the extent to which they contribute to the standard of living of their workforce and the town depends more on their social consciousness than on their ability to provide.

In societal terms providing services in this fashion is inefficient and costly: in aggregate terms, 15 per cent of the employees in enterprises are engaged in providing social ('non-productive') services; their comparable expenditures are several times greater than those of the city soviet. This is particularly the case where enterprises use their own direct labour to build accommodation. Moreover, because of the shortage of building materials, factories, instead of buying them with cash, pay with their own products, thereby perpetuating the barter economy. Building materials may be brought from other provinces (*oblasti*) or even from other republics, which increases the cost of construction still further. (Of course, the division of labour and product specialisation promoted by the planning system is responsible for these inefficient transfers.)

The direct labour method also means that construction times are protracted, the final product frequently of a low standard, and – because the housing stock of many of the older enterprises is in bad need of major refurbishment – costs generally significantly exceed those incurred by local soviets. This does not take into account the enterprise director's time: he is distracted from the more important tasks of running the factory.

The duplication, waste and irrational use of land and other resources which this situation creates is fertile soil for conflicts between city residents, labour collectives, local soviets and enterprises. Ironically perhaps, the problems arising from the systemic contradictions between the two principal planning authorities (soviets and ministries) is actually being exacerbated by the economic reforms, especially by the Law on Enterprises.[15] This allows labour collectives to determine their social priorities and protects them from interference from local government.[16] Thus, the positive advantages that inhere in the 'democratisation' process should not be allowed to conceal the difficulties that it can create. It has seen the transfer of power over urban living conditions to labour collectives which have extremely wide ranging rights. In itself, the transfer of power is not necessarily a 'bad thing'; however, under conditions of severe shortages, inflation and an unstable political situation, workers' collectives are voting for maximum reductions in the scale of capital investment in the urban infrastructure and a curtailment of all forms of aid to the town.[17] In a whole number of towns the local soviet is failing to receive from enterprises payments which are stipulated by law, and no mechanisms really exist for the soviets to recover the monies.

The problem of control is not restricted to rights over new investment, since strikers in Donetsk, for instance, have been demanding that the local soviet return to them a large proportion of the housing stock built by miners and transferred to the city. At the meeting in February 1990 of the Committee on Social and Economic Policy, one of the members, a foreman at 'Uralmash', complained that 30 per cent of the tenants in 'our housing' were not employed by Uralmash and it was only reasonable to expect their employers to contribute to the cost of the upkeep of these dwellings.[18]

Following the laws passed in 1990 on land and on property, Kicv and Moscow and a number of other cities have begun to charge differential rents depending on location, although local governments lack experience and a method for calculating the charges that they make. Their task is hampered by the fact that they are unable to pay salaries, or bonuses in otherwise unattainable consumer goods, which co-operatives or the social affairs departments of large (and rich) enterprises are able to offer in order to attract specialist labour. It is unlikely that the revenues generated from the transfer into the city budgets of the new income taxes will be sufficient to deal with the whole range of urban problems. For this to occur, it is still necessary to win over the hearts and resources of labour collectives. This will depend in part on the attitudes of the latter to their deputies and Parliament, and the degree to which they regard them as the legitimate authority.

The Supreme Soviet in the summer of 1990 was considering three draft laws concerned with the management by the republics of their economies and social affairs, local self-government and the boundaries of competence of the centre and the republics. Housing policy will inevitably be affected by the final form taken by these laws, but at a minimum they will leave the republics to decide on the housing policy which best suits their needs. In 1990, despite the passing of a series of decrees since 1957, all concerned with transferring housing to the local soviets, enterprises own half of the total urban housing stock nationwide. This figure rises to 90 per cent in new towns.

Given that there are cases where enterprises build housing, not because they have a shortage of accommodation for their workers, but because housing is a sort of 'hard currency', it seems likely that enterprise directorates or workers' collectives are not going to be very willing to surrender control over this valuable asset. *Perestroika* may have emancipated the workforce by giving them the right to the fruits of their labour; but like the famous edict of 1861, when the granting of land did not allow the peasant to move away from the village, the Soviet worker today remains tied to his workplace.

6. Social Groups, Life Chances and Access to Housing

For decades statistics on housing were produced and packaged in an extremely simple form. Essentially, every Soviet citizen knew that the housing norm which the state set as its objective was nine square metres of 'actual dwelling area' per person. Secondly, statistical handbooks, the daily press and professional journals gave the average number of square metres of 'overall living space' enjoyed by the nation's population. This figure was refined to give republic averages and the average to be found in a number of the largest cities. The considerable disparities between the Baltic republics (17.4 square metres in 1988) on the one hand, and the Central Asian republics (11.4 square metres) on the other, were visible, but they drew little comment.[19] Similarly, regional differences within the RSFSR – such as the dreadful living conditions of oil workers in the Tyumen' – were mentioned. An occasional monograph listed differences in average living space norms between oblasts. By the early 1980s more was being said about the below-average standards found in Siberia. Figures on average dwelling space were supplemented by macro-level data on the proportion of the housing stock (and new building) which was provided with a full range of amenities.

The message was clear and candidly stated: the state was diverting huge resources to trying to solve the housing problem which, though reducing, remained acute and so more must be built. The population was also frequently reminded that they enjoyed the lowest rental charges in the world. Apart from the ideological motivation and propaganda advantage of this policy, rents were kept low because of the poor quality of the housing concerned and because they served as a legitimating factor for the political system. However, recently, even the 'fact' of low rents has been denounced as a myth and propaganda.[20] With the advent of *perestroika* and *glasnost'*, the de-mythologising of the claim of low rents is associated with the 'unravelling of the average' to reveal class and ethnic differences.

The standard of *rural* housing in terms of dwelling size and level of amenity provision varies by republic. Overall, only 10–12 per cent of rural dwellings have central heating, mains water and sewage disposal, and a mere 5 per cent have hot water. Even in newly erected state accommodation in Kazakhstan, only 6 per cent of the housing is supplied with all amenities – although in the Baltic republics the figure is over 90 per cent.

The republican differences found in towns are also found in the countryside: rural families in the Baltic republics enjoy over 24 square metres of overall living space per person compared with 11 square metres in the Central Asian republics and Azerbaidzhan. (The remaining republics lie between these extremes.) While the housing stock increased everywhere, the republics in the bottom category experienced an even greater increase in their rural populations, which led to an actual decline in per capita living space in Tadzhikstan.

These regional differences have persisted. Nationwide in 1981–85, 1.8 square metres of housing was erected for each rural inhabitant. However, in Tadzhikstan and Azerbaidzhan the figure was 0.7 square metres and in Estonia 2.9 square metres. This disparity is attributed to the shortfall in state investment in these poorer regions.[21] As a general rule, the best housing is found in the regions with the strongest economies. The underlying tension which different levels of development generate has found the fissure of internal ethnic conflict through which to express itself: the substantive factor behind the alleged 'massacre' in the Fergana valley between Uzbeks and Kirghizians was the acute housing shortage. The same reason was frequently cited as an explanation for the brutal conflict between Turks and Uzbeks, and Armenian refugees and Kazakhs. As in other societies, housing is often the form in which inter-ethnic tensions make themselves apparent. It is a visible issue around which people can construct their cultural identity, which is then expressed not as an outbreak of fury against the dominant power at the central government level but as an attack upon a more tangible target – another, opposed, local community.

The growth in intraregional differences is an unintended consequence of planning policies of the 1960s and 1970s, to create within each *oblast'* a model village. Many of the houses and buildings, since they were custom designed and built and fully equipped and connected to mains systems, could cost 60–70 000 roubles for a single family dwelling.[22] But as with so many architectural models in the Soviet Union they remain models: the resources to convert villages into fleets behind these flagships have always been lacking. Until recently, porticoed palaces of culture and grandiose architectural projects were regarded as offering a positive palliative for the poverty of day-to-day living conditions.[23] Now, the negative consequences of this policy are beginning to reveal themselves. For instance, in some cases only the centre of the settlement was reconstructed. The tenants of these new homes were sometimes migrants, which caused such bad feeling among the native inhabitants, who were left in their rundown housing on the outskirts of the village, that they decided to leave.

The principal reason for mentioning this seemingly trivial social fact is to underline the wide range of social differences and tensions which have been generated in Soviet society. Strikes by miners and wage demands by other workers, frustration with the progress of *perestroika*, fears of inflation and a widespread revival of religious and cultural consciousness and identification may be seen as having their origin, at least in part, in an accumulation of housing difficulties, injustices and trauma in the past.

Differences in standards of living are acknowledged to be very high.[24] Those on high incomes are also those who receive the best health treatment, access to consumer goods and housing. According to the statistics produced by Zaichenko, which are neither better nor worse than others, the contemporary class pyramid in the Soviet Union is not so indistinguishable from that found in pre-revolutionary Russia: 'the rich' comprise 2.3 per cent of the population, 11.2 per cent fall into the middle class ('half of them owing their prosperity to illicit dealings with goods in short supply'), and the remaining 86.5 per cent are 'the poor'. This leads to the conclusion that 'We demonstrate a much higher degree of property inequality than other industrialised countries because of extremely large income brackets and a rudimentary middle class'. Accumulated savings from high incomes and perquisites associated with the office *can* mean that 'most of the special pension recipients have major personal assets (flat, car, dacha)' as well as a pension of up to 500 roubles a month.[25] At the other end of the social hierarchy are the poor. Poverty is now officially recognised. Begging and arrests for vagrancy testify to its existence. Millions of those on pensions fall underneath the poverty line, as do invalids and other low-income groups (often classified as 'people of modest means' [*maloobespechennye*]). The system does not, however, have an adequate institutional network to deal with people lacking in material provision.[26] To date, studies of social class, rather than being serious theoretical treatises on the causes and nature of inequality, tend to be descriptive denunciations of privilege which are suffused with moral indignation. In so far as their revolution was

fought in the name of an egalitarian ethos, their indignation is justified. The data does suggest the posing of two critical questions: how
does the 'socialist aristocracy' – the *nomenklatura* – transform itself
into a bourgeoisie? Secondly, what steps have to be taken in order to
protect those who will be weak in the market place? Privatisation will
not benefit everyone. The Soviet Union lacks the concepts to formu-
late the policies and the institutional mechanisms to deal with
homelessness and unemployment. After all, ideologically such
phenomena could not and did not exist under socialism. The system
coped with 'surplus labour' by overmanning, and with its acute
housing shortage by keeping space standards very low: norms were
lowered to make demand equate with supply.

The housing shortage, a virtual state monopoly of the building
industry – especially in the production of building materials – and a
centralised and bureaucratic control over housing allocation had a
crucial negative effect. They allowed those in positions of economic
and political power to reap housing privileges. The attitude towards
privileges amongst the Soviet population, as revealed by a national
random sample conducted by the All-Union Centre for the Study of
Public Opinion, admits to some confusion: 68 per cent of those
questioned thought that no one should be granted privileges; at the
same time, 29 per cent felt that, though there should be no privileges,
people could be given material rewards in the form of money, and a
slightly smaller percentage (24) believed that privileges should be
accorded to 'concrete persons' for special services rendered to society
or for outstanding achievements. As far as this paper is concerned,
the finding which is of greatest interest showed 43 per cent of the
respondents suggesting that *housing* could be used as a privilege
accorded to people with specific occupational functions – that is, the
nomenklatura.[27]

The government has thus to confront two problems: firstly, it must
remove 'unjustified' privileges such as high space standards and easy
access to housing; secondly, it has to move from providing general
subsidies for bricks and mortar subsidies to making grants to specific
groups of individuals. In doing so it can take the opportunity of
erasing some of the inequities characteristic of the existing system. If
the state subsidy is removed from public housing, then the better off
will be motivated to buy, while that remaining in the hands of the
state and accommodating low income groups will become social
housing.

As far as house building is concerned, the question is raised as to the possible appearance of private construction firms and speculative building. A private building sector has existed for some time in the form of casual labourers (*shabashniki*). But they were essentially illegal. Now builders are forming themselves into co-operatives. In other words, a private sector in the building industry does exist. Because those in the private building sector cannot buy or be allocated land on which to build, they cannot, strictly speaking, engage in speculative building: they are contracted to construct dwellings for those who have been allocated building land. A distinction has to be drawn here between those who could be responsible for new building and those who should undertake large scale urban renewal. Will foreign investors wish to redevelop the centres of St Petersburg, Kiev and Vilnius (not to mention Prague and Berlin)? If they are invited to do so, will they seek to make claims on the land on which the buildings stand and insist on purchasing the freehold? As rents rise to market levels, what effect will this have on the social profiles and desirability of particular locations?

It is within the context of these dimensions of Soviet (and now post-Soviet) society that current housing policy has to be interpreted.

THE EVOLVING STRATEGY

In February 1990, a meeting of the Committee for Social and Economic Policy of the CC CPSU addressed itself to a draft document on 'The Basic Directions of Housing Policy under Present Conditions'.[28] It noted that the acute housing shortage was causing violations of the principle of social justice in offering access to and acquisition of accommodation. The shortages experienced by the many coexisted with the enjoyment of 'additional space' by the few. The whole concept of privileged allocation of additional space at advantageous prices to a large group of senior officials employed in state enterprises and organisations, senior staff officers and leading figures in the arts and sciences, was seen as being unjustifiable. These particular privileges should be confined to those suffering from specific serious illnesses, to war invalids and to Heroes of the Soviet Union and Heroes of Soviet Labour. The positive intent in such statements about social justice pales away when such outmoded notions as rewards for 'Heroes' are maintained. The sentiment is diminished by the distinct feeling of inauthenticity: invalids and war veterans, for instance, have never fared especially well in the rush for better housing, and there are grounds for scepticism that they will fare any better in the future.

The general direction of change is that emphasised by the Second Congress of USSR People's Deputies, which recommended the decentralisation of control over the allocation of investment funds for house building and the distribution of accommodation to enterprises (work collectives) and local soviets. The finance for housing construction and maintenance should come from money earned by workers' collectives and private individuals. Decentralisation has also been taken by some to imply that the notion and practice of having a single set of rules governing housing allocation throughout the country should be abolished in favour of increasing the freedom of local soviets and enterprise to 'compile their own rules for allocating housing, which would be ratified by sessions of the Soviet and workers' collectives'.[29] A sharp shift from a system of centrally prescribed rules and norms to one granting complete autonomy to landlords will not be without its difficulties. However, this is clearly the direction in which the government is moving. Rozanov, the Chairman of the recently created State Committee on Architecture and Town Planning, which oversees all civil construction, considers that the state's role should be restricted to providing 'free accommodation' only for those families who have less than 9 square metres per person, are sharing accommodation, or are living in substandard conditions. Most housing should be built at the expense of individuals themselves, so that finally a situation will be reached where housing becomes a commodity (*zhil'e stat' tovarom*).

The substance of this document, according to a decree (*Ukaz*) issued by the (then) President of the Soviet Union,[30] must include changes to ensure a doubling in output of dwelling. This will require a fundamental change in investment policy in house building and a redistribution of capital investment from the construction of factories (and other forms of 'productive activity') to house building. The *Ukaz* requires an expansion in the sources of finance by drawing upon 'state, leasing and co-operative enterprises, share societies (*aktsionernye obshchestva*), voluntary organisations, bank loans and personal savings and by building housing for sale with low monthly repayments spread out over a long period. This is to be accompanied by the establishment of a network of commercial banks, building co-operatives and firms dealing with the sale and renting of accommodation'.

But neither an expansion in the 'financial base' nor an increase in the output of material and equipment by existing enterprises will be sufficient to reach the goals set. In addition, machine tool manufacturers will have to convert to produce for the building industry instead of for defence purposes. In order to assist the conversion, tax concessions will be granted to enterprises (regardless of their property form) producing materials and equipment for housing and civic construction. Building organisations are to be encouraged to adopt 'progressive' management practices which will entail placing state enterprises on leasing arrangements and converting them into shareholding societies. The structure of imports will also have to be examined in order that imports will be able to contribute to the modernisation of the building industry.

Despite the fact that the state's policy has for long been to transfer housing from enterprises to the local soviet, and despite the criticisms which have been directed at this form of tenure – which has the effect of creating an 'enserfed' workforce – the decree stipulates that the role played by employers in providing their workforces with accommodation should be increased both directly and indirectly by, for instance, offering interest free loans and grants to workers wishing to acquire their own housing. At the same time, enhancing the role of enterprises naturally carries a number of implications. Firstly, it reduces the central budget's contribution to housing provision and in doing so represents a radical change in the way in which housing is financed. At present the profit tax is a major source of central government revenue which is then reallocated through the budget to various ministries and then down the chain of command to enterprises, to be spent on housing. Secondly, by abolishing this system, a direct link will be seen as having been established between those responsible for making profits and those benefiting from them. However, the necessary outcome of making this the axle between production and consumption is to make the rich richer – unless other redistributive tax policies are introduced. It also makes clear that the state's responsibility is to be confined to meeting the needs of those who are not in the profit-making sectors. On the other hand, it does counter criticisms levelled by conservatives, who are resentful of privatisation of the housing stock and who prefer basic social needs to be met by 'collectives of workers'. It is difficult to be certain that distribution by 'workers' collectives' or a committee created by them will ensure social justice in the allocation of accommodation.

The decree reiterated the sentiments of the decree of February 1988, that the negative attitudes toward building for owner-occupation have to be overcome in order for output in this sector to register a sharp increase. As the deputy chairman of the State Building Committee (*Gosstroi*) noted a few days after the issuing of the *Ukaz*, 'our hopes for finding a way out of the crisis rest with the private sector'. The change in attitude would then see plots of land being allocated for building, sites cleared, infrastructure provided and the right to ownership, use, disposal and hereditary transfer guaranteed. Greater priority has simultaneously to be given to the diversification of the forms and conditions for granting loans for private building. Priority has also to be accorded to firms created with the specific purpose of supplying the private builder with materials for purchase and plant for hire. In order to ensure high quality standards in this sector, the decree called for further encouragement to be given to the creation of design consultancies – although, in fact, this represents one of the fastest growing spheres of activity in the co-operative movement. Another innovation inserted into the decree is that architects are allowed to design different types of houses within a range of prices.

In this 'regulated market' phase, which places emphasis on solving the housing problem principally through private individuals (and co-operatives) and work collectives, the state's role is to concentrate on actually increasing the aid that it gives to a whole range of disadvantaged social groups. As well as those already mentioned, specific reference was made to 'families of men in the armed forces and of those demobilised as part of the government's policy of reducing the size of the army on the grounds that they form a "political category" whose standard of living has been adversely affected' by the outbreak of peace and goodwill in Europe. A second category requiring state assistance embraces 'teachers, doctors and other workers in the "non-productive" sphere as well as families on low incomes'. (In fact, membership of the two groups overlaps or directly coincides: those in the non-productive sphere have traditionally had low incomes. With the growth of a legal second economy, of co-operatives and of the number of organisations which are self-financing and paying their employees higher incomes, the nexus is no longer so true.)

As far as the problems faced by younger people in trying to obtain accommodation are concerned, the *Ukaz* recommended that young families are to be helped to build their own homes and housing complexes, and that co-operatives and hostels are to be built for young adults and young families. The extensive reliance placed on self-build by young people is still attractive, for although the heroic period of the building of socialism has passed, the concrete construction of one's home is for many young people the only way in which they can acquire a place of their own.

The *Ukaz* specifically refers to the formation of a housing market in which every individual may freely acquire a flat or house through purchase, taking out a long lease or renting in the public sector. This will require removing all unnecessary restrictions on the reallocation and exchange of accommodation. Individuals with more living space than they require must be given an incentive to transfer to a smaller flat by offering them financial compensation. The establishment of a housing market also requires a simplifying of the procedures and methods for exchanging accommodation. The issue of flat exchange was the most common cause, in the experience of Alexandra Biryukova, former Chairman of the Central Committee Department for Social Development, for members of her constituency visiting her surgery. Because officials of the various executive committees paid scant attention to flat exchanges, 'fixers' (*maklery*) emerged to fill the gap. Today they are charging 700–1000 roubles for each square metre of additional space for which they help to arrange an exchange. This move towards the creation of a housing market embodies the decrees already mentioned which allow local soviets, enterprises and house-building (and other) co-operatives to convert their properties into owner occupation.

A major step along the path of privatisation and towards the formation of a housing market was taken in July 1990 when the Moscow City Soviet decided to allow Muscovites to buy and sell their flats. The transfer was to begin in 1991, with details on how property was to be transferred being issued in September 1990. Deputies justified their policy on the basis of an argument that had been circulating for some time, namely that each Soviet citizen had long paid for the cost of his flat, and since each Muscovite occupied about 12 square metres of space, this would be presented to them free of charge. The surplus would be paid for at a rate yet to be determined by building economists; the rate being mentioned, ranging from 50 to 200 roubles, was said to lack any foundation. Mossovet also decided to establish a special 'stock exchange' to help individuals dispose of flats which were previously state property and now owned by their former sitting tenants.[31] This is a harbinger for the creation of a housing market which in time will come to acquire (even if it does not require) the whole complex of institutions so familiar in the West, such as estate agents, conveyancers and credit and finance organisations to create a proper housing market.

Another interesting innovative idea which is part of this radical package of housing reforms entails providing compensation for those inhabiting less than 12 square metres per person. This will take the form not of money but 'apartment cheques', issued for each square metre under quota. These securities will actually become the commitment of the municipality to pay the citizen for the purchase of a new flat through the 'stock exchange'. Then, since the apartment cheques will represent floor space and not a fixed monetary value, the real value of the cheques will increase with demand and be inflation proof. Finally, and predictably given the logic of the direction of change towards 'greater reliance on payments for services' first mooted at the XXVI Party Congress in 1981, a clause announced that the use of public utilities must gradually be paid for at a commercial rate.

CONCLUSION

Mr Gorbachev has during his incumbency been a vociferous champion of local soviets. The demand that they, as the 'local organs of power', should be the sole owners of public housing has a functional and moral appeal. Functionally, it could lead to a more rational and efficient housing construction policy. Morally, it could result in a more just distribution of accommodation, both for those in need and those who merit receiving better housing. However, not everyone sees the solution to the problem of the production and distribution of housing deriving from concentrating the control over housing in the hands of the local soviets. Media scandals and revelations about their misdemeanours in the distribution of accommodation hardly presents them as paragons of civic virtue. It is unlikely that this would be a long-term management solution. In time they will probably have to divest themselves of some responsibility for at least part of the vast housing stock that already forms part of their domain.

It is not altogether clear whether the carrot being offered to tenants in state housing – that they may purchase their property at a heavy discount – is sufficiently attractive to Soviet citizens. Their attitude resembles that of the Russian peasants on their emancipation in 1861: the land is ours, why should we now pay for it (in redemption dues)? It is being suggested that the state simply present tenants with a 'gift' of their flat. A frequently expressed objection to purchasing the property is that, because the accommodation is so bad and people have had to suffer years of waiting in the queue for accommodation whilst sharing overcrowded flats, the state has no right to suggest that any payment at all be made. In any case, so it is reasoned, tenants have, through the rental payments which they have made over time, covered the original costs of construction. Therefore, the flats are really the property of their tenants who should be given the title of owners. Morally, they should be given full proprietorship of the flats and houses. There has been some movement towards accepting this view. For instance, the meeting of the Central Committee which discussed housing policy agreed that 'old and small state flats could be transferred into the private ownership of their tenants' – as long as the new 'owners' took responsibility for care and maintenance.

The December 1988 decree proposing the selling of state flats to sitting tenants at huge discounts seemed rash, poorly conceived and a panic response to the housing crisis. The decision by Mossovet in July 1990 could be a calculated gamble in order to achieve the objective of creating a 'legitimate housing market' which, according to Osovtsov, the chairman of Mossovet's Social Policy Committee, 'alone can help solve the housing shortage, one of the most acute problems in Moscow'. Some people might sell and reap a quick gain and use the money to build a 'house in the country'. This could have the effect of stimulating the whole house construction industry. In fact, this act by Mossovet is an example of the use of a loosely formulated decree to find a way of simultaneously releasing market forces, human creativity, enterprise and the society's 'hidden reserves'. The prudent might accept the gift and then hold on to their real estate asset as a hedge against rising inflation, which would be like placing money under the mattress as far as the economy is concerned. Other outcomes are also possible.

In short, changes are now to be introduced in the system of rental payments in the public sector. Families on low incomes or living in substandard accommodation should be given rent-free accommodation. Individuals in self-contained dwellings are almost certainly going to be required to pay a rent which reflects its size and quality and are to face higher charges for their 'surplus' space. Considering the general hostility towards the housing privileges enjoyed by high status groups, following a review of the whole system, it is likely that privileges of this kind will be largely abolished. At the same time there seems to be widespread support for taking steps to protect weak and vulnerable groups. This is associated with a general acceptance of the need to introduce differential rents to reflect the quality and location of the housing.

However, as indicated above, there does seem to be a groundswell of hostility amongst tenants about the propriety of 'selling tenants their own flats' and also about the charging of higher rents. These attitudes towards (higher) charges for accommodation find reflection in the large number of people who fail to pay even the low rents which are presently being charged. Rent arrears in Leningrad (now St Petersburg), for instance, are extremely high. As the chairman of the Leningrad city soviet observed, however, since nothing can be done to retrieve the rent owed before differential rents are introduced, clearly defined laws must be introduced in this policy area.[32] Under these circumstances, giving away state-owned accommodation might be a rational solution. Yet to do so might delay the day when Soviet citizens understand the notion of the 'market'.

Finally, it has to be recognised that a strong strain of egalitarianism runs through the society. Many still adhere to the belief in a 'universal housing norm' which everyone should enjoy. This might be perpetuated by the system of making enterprises responsible for financing house construction, since it preserves a collectivist mode of allocating resources. Allowing co-operative members to dispose of their flats when they have finished paying for them, stimulating the owner-occupied sector and finding ways of facilitating the exchange of property might, in cultivating a market mentality, act as a counter to the enterprise-controlled sector, eventually drawing it into the market arena.

Notes

1. 'Many do not understand that the market exists outside politics . . . it was and is part of us in the form of a shadow [*tenevoi*]. But in general the market [*rynok*] is the means for the functioning of the economy. If we say: "more democracy" – then in the economy, democracy is the market.' 'V ekonomike demokratiya – eto rynok', *Argumenty i fakty*, no. 22, 2–8 July 1990.
2. TsNIIEP zhilishcha, *General'naya skhema obsepecheniya k 2000 godu kazhdoi sovetskoi sem'i otdel'noi kvartiroi ili individual'nym domom* (Moscow, 1988) p. 10.
3. A resolution passed by the 9th session of the USSR Supreme Soviet in

May 1988 acknowledged that it would be necessary to build more than the earlier forecast 2.2–2.3 billion square metres by the year 2000. Cited in ibid., p. 11.
4. M. Krushinskii, 'Zaprety snyaty', *Izvestiya*, 24 May 1990.
5. Gos. Kom po arkhitektury i gradostroitel'stva pri Gosstroya SSSR, *Kontseptsiya gosudarstvennoi zhilishchnoi politiki SSSR do 2000 goda* (Moscow, 1990).
6. B. Kolotilkin, 'Dreams of Home', *Arguments and Facts International*, October–November 1989, p. 10.
7. G. Andrusz, *Housing and Urban Development in the USSR* (London: Macmillan, 1984).
8. 'O merakh po uskoreniyu razvitiya individual'nogo zhilishchnogo stroitel'stva', *SP SSSR*, 1988, no. 11, art. 28.
9. 'O merakh po uskoreniyu razvitiya zhilishchnoi kooperatsii', *SP SSSR*, 1988, no. 16, art. 43.
10. O. Bessonova, 'K voprosu o kvartirnoi plate v SSSR', *Ekonomika i prikladnaya sotsiologiya*, no. 1, 1988.
11. E. Rozanov, 'Kvartiru na prodazhu', *Pravda*, 12 December 1988.
12. V Kommissiyakh TsK KPSS, 'Ob osnovnykh napravleniyakh zhilishchnoi politiki v sovremennykh usloviyakh', *Izvestiya TsK KPSS*, no. 3, 1990.
13. G. Andrusz, 'Moscow Conference Report 1: The Re-emergence of Soviet Sociology', *International Journal of Urban and Regional Sociology*, vol. 14, no. 2, 1990.
14. N. Alekseev, *Ekonomicheskii eksperiment. Sotsial'nye aspekty* (Moscow, 1987) p. 187.
15. V. Laptev, 'Zakon o predpriyatii i khozyaistvennoe zakonodatel'stvo', *Khozyaistvo i pravo*, no. 6, 1989.
16. Local residents campaigning for the closure of ecologically damaging factories are facing considerable opposition from the employees of factories which have transferred on to the new system of economic accounting. They are unwilling to introduce technology which could adversely affect current revenues, preferring instead to pay themselves higher salaries and spend money on social projects which directly benefit them. In fact, work collectives are going on to the offensive. Their response to demands that certain workshops should be closed down on environmental grounds has been to lay claims at the door of the local government over a whole range of social issues.
17. See, for example, V. Maslennikov, 'Organy vlasti i trudovye kollektivy', *Sovety narodnykh deputatov*, no. 10, 1989.
18. *Izvestiya TsK KPSS*, no. 3, 1990, p. 10.
19. *Narodnoe khozyaistvo SSSR v 1988 g.* (Moscow, 1989) p. 168.
20. O. Bessonova, 'Sovetskaya model' zhilishchnykh otnoshenii: Genezis, suchnost' i puti perestroiki', *AN SSSR SO. IEiOPP* (Novosibirsk, 1988); G. Andrusz, 'A Note on the Financing of Housing in the Soviet Union', *Soviet Studies*, vol. 42, no. 3, July 1990.
21. T. Belkina, 'Sel'skii zhilishchnyi fond: sostoyanie i perspektivy razvitiya', *Zhilishchnoe i kommunal'noe khozyaistvo*, no. 1, January 1990.
22. Ibid.

23. G. Andrusz, 'The Soviet Built Environment in Theory and Practice', *International Journal of Urban and Regional Research*, vol. 11, no. 4, 1987.
24. A. Zaichenko, 'A Wealth of Privilege', *Arguments and Facts International*, vol. 1, no. 1, January 1990.
25. Ibid. This has to be compared with the average monthly salary of 220 roubles a month and an average monthly pension of 80 roubles.
26. In the first six months of 1989, 660 people were detained in Moscow for vagrancy and were assisted by the militia rather than a social service department. The first soup kitchen – evidence of a nascent voluntary sector with charitable status – has emerged in Moscow. E. Valyuzhenikh, 'Begging the Question', *Arguments and Facts International*, vol. 1, no. 2, February 1990.
27. I am grateful to Svetlana Sydorenko for allowing me to see the results of a public opinion survey.
28. *Izvestiya TsK KPSS*, no. 3, 1990.
29. Ibid., p. 10.
30. 'O novykh pokhodakh k resheniyu zhilishchnoi problemy v strane i merakh po ikh prakticheskoi realizatsii', *Izvestiya*, 20 May 1990.
31. *Moscow News*, no. 28, 22–29 July 1990, p. 2.
32. *Izvestiya TsK KPSS*, no. 3, 1990, p. 18.

2 The Soviet Union's New Co-operatives: Goals and Accomplishments

Lars Ohlsson

The decision in favour of the new co-operatives was first mooted at the XXVII Congress of the CPSU in 1986, where the need was expressed for a general revision of the existing economic principles.[1] Towards this end, in November 1986 a Law on Individual Labour Activity was passed, and statutes covering four forms of co-operative activity followed in February 1987.[2] Finally, a Law on Co-operatives was passed in May 1988.[3] This formative stage of co-operation was characterised by clashes between the command economy and the new co-operatives. Relations between the co-operators and the administration were also deeply affected and traditional economic and social values brought into question.

It had been intended that the co-operatives would be self-administering units, operating outside state administrative control and organised in a non-hierarchical way. The members would be real owners, conducting their own internal affairs, and with the right to decide upon co-operative property, prices and distribution of income within the limits of the law. The departure from existing principles was remarkable in four respects: independence from state administration, market orientation, economic self-administration and internal democracy. Labour could be hired on a contractual basis. The differences between the new and the old co-operatives were emphasised.[4]

Although the avowed goals of the new system were economic and social, there were also obvious political implications. Co-operation was to be a test bed for new principles, which should gradually imprint themselves upon the whole economic and administrative mechanism. The co-operatives would be an attractive example of high productivity and market adaptation, which would compete with state production. The new system was also intended to encourage a switch of personal savings to the production sector and the diversion of money from the shadow economy. Production, primarily of

27

consumer goods and services, was to be small-scale, with reliance on local resources and reserves of labour.[5] The new co-operation was described as a step towards a market-oriented socialism, a form of collective property equal to state property.

Given the fact that the economic and administrative environment had not been adapted to accommodate the co-operatives, the decision in favour of the latter might be seen to be as unrealistic as it was bold. It was subsequently argued that if an all-round transformation, or substantial parts of it, had occurred from the first, the results would have been more in line with expectations and the co-operators would have had a fairer chance of success.[6] However, resistance and unfavourable structural conditions, especially with respect to trade in the means of production and the conditions laid down for contractual agreements between producers, proved a great hindrance.

INDEPENDENCE AND REGULATION

Freedom from administrative command has been as crucial for co-operators as their material interests. Fear of all regulation has been a recurrent theme in the debates on co-operation,[7] for it has been seen as an instrument with a multiplicity of repressive effects in the hands of the bureaucracy. The fate of previous forms of independent organisation is also well remembered.[8] The issue of regulation has, indeed, been presented as nothing less than a matter of life and death, leaving the political actors hesitant or reluctant to use it.

The original restrictions on co-operatives were left to the local authorities to implement, and they related principally to branches and categories.[9] The 1988 Law on Co-operatives was a victory for co-operative interests, in that restrictions on employment and recruitment were lifted; the field of activity became virtually unlimited and the registration procedure was reduced to being almost a formality. In effect, any regulation would be the result of economic activity and legal requirement.[10] However, with the co-operators still beset by problems arising from the command system, legal limitations and a still predominant bureaucracy, independence remains a goal yet to be achieved.

As was noted above, the executive committees of the local soviets were charged with applying the regulations, but they were also entrusted with the task of stimulating, supporting, and giving advice on co-operative affairs: specifically, they were to facilitate supplies, give information on the structure of demand, and advise on bureaucratic formalities. Much scope was left for adaptation and discretion, in effect implying that local attitudes and initiatives were to be decisive. Central control was only to be invoked in the event of outright refusal to obey the regulations.[11]

Legal regulation has been very much affected by previous discrepancies between the law and its practical application, by distortions resulting from unclear and contradictory provisions, by sub-legal enactments cancelling out laws, and by legal requirements not being made public. The Law on Co-operatives was at first considered an adequate instrument, but its shortcomings soon became evident, and local practices began to develop in other directions. Indeed, by 1989 it was already being claimed that the law was obsolete.[12] Nonetheless, the legal situation has given the co-operators certain advantages, especially in regard to taxes, price policy and choice of branches. On the other hand, the bureaucracy has retained its superiority by being able to control decision-making in general and distribution of material assets in particular. The benefits extolled by national policy makers have been usurped by local bureaucracies. Co-operation has been forced in undesirable directions, and co-operators have had recourse to methods which have resulted in conflicts, leaving the system all the more weakened.

The traditional method of intervention through the party organs or activists has either not been used or the agents have simply refused to act. The latter have remained indifferent both to national priorities and to co-operative and bureaucratic abuse of the regulations. When they have acted, they have sided with the local bureaucracy, which indicates either uncertainty as to their role or the pressure of a social environment stronger than party command.[13]

The social actors have pulled in different directions, in accordance with the amount of power or pressure at their disposal. Recent criticism of the practical results sees any failures as stemming from an inadequate use of the available legal and economic instruments.[14] While inexperience and incompetence have undoubtedly contributed, ambiguities in the regulations have played no small part. Again, stimulation without regulation has given co-operation a dynamic but rough-hewn character. Stricter regulation, however, would have been taken advantage of by the bureaucracy. Thus, basic social and economic conflict was an inevitable obstacle.

ECONOMIC AND ADMINISTRATIVE STRUCTURE

Since the command system determines the pattern of distribution of resources and the relations between central and local levels of administration, there are strict limits to the resources at the free disposal of state enterprises and local administrations. This system determines the behaviour of the actors by the distribution of competence, tasks, and resources, and also by establishing certain practices and internalising values and interests.

The local bureaucracies of Soviet organs and enterprises have traditionally been the disposers or mediators of resources, which are and were ever scarce and accessible only through that mediation. This has defined their immediate interests and their power. Co-operators, searching for access to supplies, have been forced to go through bureaucratic bodies which will claim plan priority, either real or imagined. Such a situation was always bound to lead to tensions in the procuring of inputs for co-operative activities, since the bureaucracy could be expected to react negatively to the demands of this new form of independent activity. The bureaucratic apparatus not only controlled supplies but could introduce obstacles at will in the form of additional formalities and documentation. However, these might also be the result of real obligations under the new legislation or surviving practices of the old.[15] The co-operators had expected freedom from administrative tutelage, and on encountering the contrary they became angry and spiteful. Conflict with the command economy affected behaviour and attitudes by sowing suspicion and distrust.

The command system has led to local bureaucracies and enterprise managements developing their own ways and means of production and distribution. To the co-operative sector such informal and illegal elements of the shadow economy have actually been important sources of supplies of all kinds, including capital, and in providing entrepreneurs, always in short supply among a population characterised by passivity and inexperience in business. The new co-operatives have served to legalise parts of the shadow economy, and have integrated hidden resources into open production, linking them in a better way to the national economy. If the shadow economy has been of service to co-operators it has also exerted some degree of pressure upon them. As the co-operators sought additional resources, 'black' money was on the lookout for profitable and legal investment opportunities; dependency relations developed quickly.

The potential advantages were considered, but it seems that the potential negative effects were not.

The close relationship between *perestroika* and co-operation has often been stated, in that the same economic principles have guided the progress of both. Where *glasnost'* has had the effect of diverting attacks away from the co-operatives, radicals have intervened in the debate on the side of the latter in the matter of principle and in event of local hostility. Members of the professions, including scientists, have played an important role as advisers. The economic and administrative transformations have, however, been slow and of little impact, leaving the position of local bureaucracy largely unaffected.

The structural conflicts between the command economy, the shadow economy and *perestroika* have to some degree been aggravated by the partial dissolution of the old structures, with such effects as open defiance by bureaucracy of elements of the new structure, controversy about regulations and the division of administrative responsibility, and all resulting in weakened control and more discretion in the hands of the local authorities.

ISSUES OF CONFLICT

The demands of the new co-operatives were for premises, machinery, raw materials, capital and labour. Since distribution of supplies was restricted to the command economy and at non-market prices, it was inevitable that the demands for inputs of the new co-operatives would provoke conflicts over what they might sell, at what prices, and how trade should be organised. Scarcity was part of the problem, but there was also the question of who was to be in control and whose interests were being affected. Centrally and locally controlled resources raised different problems, and substantial differences arose depending upon whether supplies were obtained from the planned sector, from the illegal sector or obtained illegally from the planned sector.

While legal supplies were obtainable from the state supply agency (*Gossnab*) and from individual enterprises, the process was complicated by the need to get the approval of ministries and executive committees. Such negotiations have proved to be tiresome, time consuming and of uncertain outcome. Even when resources have been abundant, the practice has been to conceal them, represent them as scarce and make them available to the co-operatives only at high cost;[16] there are reports of cases where access has been refused to resources which are plentiful and officially open.[17] It would appear from the evidence that access has depended more on the say-so of individual functionaries than on the availability of supplies or on formal regulations. Thus, resources are obtained mostly through having the right contacts and using the proper approach to those in command: local state organs, banks, state enterprises and 'branches' of the shadow economy, with the local bureaucrats of the executive committees as the key actors.

Although disposing of limited resources, local officials of this kind have shown themselves unwilling to help co-operators when they have acted as mediators between enterprises and co-operatives. There have been frequent accusations of corruption and extortion.[18] The impression is given that the bureaucrats routinely augment their income through money obtained in such ways from the co-operatives.

Capital in the form of credits is also reported to be subject to the will of individual bank chiefs. It is not always possible to insist upon one's rights, and recourse is had to bribes. Criticism of bank chiefs made by sources even outside the co-operative movement has also focused attention on the practice of approving credits without a proper scrutiny of financial plans and without checking on the background of the co-operator concerned.[19] Even when credit has been approved, little effective financial control is exercised, with instances of large credits not being paid back.[20] Bribes have made permission all the more easy to obtain and control all the more lenient.

Although enterprises command the resources, premises, machinery, raw materials and often the right to accept tenants, and the co-operatives in their turn are free to link up with them, this has not been the optimum solution. The pattern has been of the co-operative turning its face away from the market and adapting its production to the needs of the enterprise and to state orders (*goszakazy*). Even the fact that in such circumstances co-operators are subject to fixed prices for state supplies has not been a problem for them, however much it is for the promoters of the reforms. Although the profits might be smaller, they are nonetheless secure. The problem for the enterprise, the co-operatives and the state lies in this 'unharmonious' symbiosis with, for example, its unwanted competition for labour.

Supplies are also obtained by co-operatives from the state retail network of shops and markets, and these tend to be lacking in quantity and assortment, and consist mainly of foodstuffs, household goods and tools. Even here, co-operatives are restricted in the amounts which they can buy.[21] Where co-operators have breached such restrictions, they have been accused of 'draining the market'.

In general, co-operative needs are satisfied in legal ways, but recourse must at times be had to informal or illegal methods and sources. The situation has improved by regulations being made more clear with respect to co-operators' rights, and by a reduction in the restrictions on the sale of used machinery and the selling-off of state property.[22] Nonetheless, the delay in establishing a wholesale trade in the means of production has arguably been fatal to co-operation and to the environment in which it operates.[23] In the existing monopoly situation prices have been increased arbitrarily, with additional high costs to co-operatives from their having to pay bribes.

As noted above, the supply system has been the source of conflict and distortions of several kinds. Firstly, the illegal methods of procuring supplies have led to increased economic crime. Secondly, the linking up with state enterprises has led the co-operatives away from the market and into sectors which have little interest for the public. Thirdly, the 'open' market has suffered due to co-operative purchases. Fourthly, the supply situation has contributed to insecurity, which encourages maximisation of incomes, itself a source of further conflict. Fixed property has been liquidated, which has tended to increase inflation. Finally, increased costs have resulted in a price spiral with state prices raised in proportion to the higher prices of the co-operatives and vice versa.[24] Higher costs have also been the result of using illegal methods and channels of supply procurement, while illegalities have attracted the interference of the bureaucracy. Activity which depends upon illegal methods is indefensible, even if the co-operatives have been largely unable to satisfy their needs otherwise.

COOPERATION AND THE LOCAL BUREAUCRACY

In the oft-stated conflict with bureaucracy, the specific branches most referred to are the executive committees of the soviets, enterprise managements, and local functionaries directly subordinate to the central authorities. The higher bureaucracy, which is not involved in co-operative work or concerned with its immediate effects, has other interests and other devices at its disposal. Thus, the levels of bureaucracy are identifiable by the resources at their command, by the kind of control or supervision under which they work, and also the degree to which they are susceptible to pressure from above, from co-operators and from the public. These distinctions decide what attitudes and behaviour they adopt vis-à-vis the co-operatives and also how they in turn are approached by the co-operators.

Co-operators are increasingly perceived as the 'deadly enemy of the bureaucracy',[25] while the latter, at first somewhat reticent, have over the last year or so become more outspoken in their negative criticism.[26] The bureaucrats have, however, had the power to shape the co-operatives to their will, while meeting only verbal resistance.

Bad relations are caused not only by the will to damage but also by ignorance and by conflicting tasks and conduct. The bureaucrats have been appointed to dispose of resources distributed from above, while the co-operators have had to fulfil demands without free access to resources without previous experience of the market. Co-operators counter complaints of scarcities, of overburdening of official channels and lack of knowledge, with charges of bureaucratic passivity and incompetence.[27] Antagonism has also arisen as a result of the pressure of cooperators' demands for resources and more openness (*glasnost'*), the latter with the support of the mass media. The inferior administrative and economic position of the co-operators has not rendered them entirely defenceless, since they are often well-educated and enjoy the support of the intelligentsia and the political leadership. Often, hostility towards co-operatives is aroused more by the way in they appear to represent all the shortcomings of *perestroika* than by their actual activities.

When a local administration has wanted to disrupt co-operative operations, it has had sufficient means at its disposal.[28] Examples are numerous of co-operatives being prevented from registering and not having their basic demands met.[29] Again, co-operatives have been closed on the pretext that it was in the best interests of the people, rather than a matter of the law.[30] Higher authorities have not made effective sanctions available against bureaucratic arbitrariness.

Despite such antagonisms, there have been frequent reports of friendly relations and mutual support. The bureaucracy is not unmindful of the useful contribution of co-operatives to the local budget.[31] The co-operatives have also mobilised support from among enterprise managers, who have sometimes been sufficiently influential as to change the behaviour if not the attitudes of those around them. Peaceful co-existence, therefore, has been based upon mutual advantage, implying that services and 'friendship' have been bought. Any conflicts are then hidden under cover of illegal agreements. In a poll, 80 000 co-operators were asked who extorted most money from them; 30 per cent accused the functionaries of the local executive committees, while 7 per cent named racketeers.[32]

On the one hand, bureaucratic passivity and incompetence might well confer advantages on the co-operatives, especially where the sanctions or controls with respect to legal control, tax inspection and approval of credits have been called for but not actually imposed. On the other hand, such occasional benefits are counterbalanced by, for example, the increased vulnerability of the co-operatives due to their closer attachment to the illegal sector.

The traditionally estranged relations between the population and a local adminstration whose tasks are set and cadres appointed from above is changing. The latter must now be more attentive to public opinion, and in consequence become more susceptible to pressure from popular interests. Real elections have given the public greater influence and left the administration with less power. It might, therefore, be concluded from this that the co-operatives are in a more advantageous position, but the evidence suggests otherwise. Indeed, it would appear that functionaries have become even more obstructive, due to the comparative unpopularity of co-operatives among the public.[33] In addition, fear of accusations of corruption has hindered support for the co-operatives;[34] press reports have even suggested that prior to the March 1990 elections executive committees closed some co-operatives in order to gain popularity.[35]

Conflicts with bureaucracy have antagonised all sorts of organisations, and small co-operatives, in particular, are demanding to be set free of restrictions. Added impetus has been given by the lengthy process of organisation of co-operation and conflicts on the issue within the movement itself. The conflicts have also resulted in delayed growth of co-operation, a general sense of insecurity, and a greater readiness to resort to illegal methods. Disappointment at the failure of higher authorities to act against the high-handed behaviour of their subordinates in the localities, and the lack of radical measures to reform entrenched bureaucracy have also turned co-operators against *perestroika* which they often see to be slow and, in general, not to be trusted.

CO-OPERATION AND THE STATE ENTERPRISES

The association of co-operatives with state enterprises, permitting conditions to be contractually negotiated between the two partners, has often been the saving of co-operation in an otherwise hostile world.[36] The most conspicuous advantages for the co-operatives have been in common use of premises, availability of enterprise machinery, and deliveries of raw materials through state channels. Enterprise managements have, in their turn, benefited from rents and fees and the contributions of the co-operatives to plan fulfilment.[37]

Nonetheless, the usually friendly relations between enterprise managements and the co-operatives are still fragile and can too easily turn to hostility. Disputes can arise from differences in production methods and relative incomes, and also from competition for labour. Productivity has been estimated to be two to three times higher in the co-operatives, due mainly to greater labour efficiency brought about by a combination of stricter discipline and higher wages. Latecoming, drunkenness, and the other disciplinary problems so common in state enterprises are punished with dismissal in the co-operatives.[38] This has been made possible by the fact that co-operative jobs are so sought after; similar disciplinary measures are not permitted in the state sector. The higher income of the co-operative sector is the result not only of greater productivity, but also of tax benefits, low administration costs and the right to independent decision-making in respect of wages and investment allocations. In fact, the percentage investment in the co-operative sector is 25–35 per cent of earnings in comparison with around 70 per cent in the state sector. As the situation was not created by state enterprise managements, it cannot be solved by them.

Not only have such differences created bad relations between the two sectors, they have also stiffened competition for labour.[39] The co-operatives have been able to recruit a better-educated and more skilled workforce,[40] and have managed to contract a greater number of part-time workers,[41] producing a higher quantity and quality of output, than the state enterprises have been able to do.[42] Given the relatively weak legal standing of co-operatives, conflicts can often result in cancellation of contracts by enterprises.[43]

Any negative reaction on the part of state enterprise managements is not to be compared to the outright resistance of the state bureaucracy to co-operation as such. The conflicts are merely the consequence of two production units having to operate in tandem but under different sets of conditions. The demand of enterprise managements is for equal conditions and, in particular, increased wages for workers in the state sector.[44]

While the conflicts make for insecurity, an unwillingness to invest, and higher wage demands, all viewed with apprehension by the state,[45] there are cases of some sections of enterprises and even whole enterprises being transformed into co-operatives.[46] The results have been better exploitation of production resources, improved work discipline and higher productivity. There has also been a decrease in illegal activities, and supplies obtained with fewer disputes. On the negative side, co-operatives have only been partly integrated into the state economy, leaving the old system only slightly modified.

SOCIAL CONFLICT

Popular criticism is not only directed against the actual practices of the co-operative system (especially in public catering, retail trade and mediation services[47]), but often questions its very principles. Such criticisms, however, emanate mostly from those sections of the population who do not buy co-operative goods or use its services.[48]

The ideological objection focuses on the allegedly exploitative market mechanism, and attendant social injustice.[49] It has also become one part of a wider political debate joined with especial vigour by the conservative opposition. The greater the polarisation between the 'radical' and 'conservative' forces, the more strident such criticism becomes.[50]

The more explicit criticisms point to high prices for consumers and high incomes for co-operators, low quality products and services, and increased crime. The press, especially since 1989,[51] has been replete with reports of the exploitation, speculation and abuses of the co-operatives.[52] As the critics have become all-the-more scathing, the defenders of the co-operatives have been increasingly reticent.

The debate, often emotional, exaggerated and even slanderous,[53] has settled upon three main issues: the high incomes of the co-operators, the diversion of goods from the state retail market, and speculation by co-operators engaged in retailing and mediation. The co-operators insist that the relatively high incomes generated by free prices and the various other phenomena are the consequence of the operation of the laws of the market, and that criticisms are in any event invariably motivated by envy.[54] In addition, 'radical' economists argue that in the conditions of a distorted market and an unbalanced economy, transitional conflicts are an inevitability which must be endured.[55] In the course of a recent debate, co-operators were accused of buying the friendship and even the protection of administrators, banks and police, as well as that of journalists, scientists and even of people's deputies.[56] The co-operators retorted they were being made the scapegoat for an economic situation of which they, too, were the victims.

The dispute over social justice versus the market mechanism, where there are scarcities of goods and services, is, perhaps, most vexed when it relates to health care. One proponent of the co-operatives disputes the assertion that deterioration in the health service has been caused by a flight of personnel from the state health sector. Indeed, any impact made by the small share of co-operatives in this sector, he maintains, has been to ensure greater equality of access.[57]

One commentator has suggested that what few instances there have been of, for example, the diversion of goods from the state retail sector, their slight modification and sale at several times the original price, have been magnified in order to provide the pretext for conflict.[58] A veritable 'wave' of criticism of the co-operative system has been deliberately exploited by the 'conservative' camp to discredit *perestroika* as a betrayal of socialism,[59] and has allowed pressure to be put upon the policy makers who decide the fate of the co-operatives. In this way co-operation has become the whipping boy for every social contradiction and the rallying point of opinions for and against *perestroika*.

Sentiments against co-operatives, whether justified or not, have been used to legitimate negative treatment, including local restrictions and prohibitions. Despite protests, this has been a comparatively popular policy. The effect has been to restrict the development of co-operation,[60] and to impose stress on workers and even physical risk.[61]

THE SHADOW ECONOMY

The shadow economy used to embrace a substantial part of the Soviet economy in the form of informal and occasionally, but not always, illegal re-distribution and production within the state sector. However, in the last few years such activity has intensified with the transfer of property from state to group or individual ownership, and has brought with it new forms of illegality.[62]

Independent co-operatives and individual labour activity have unintentionally led to increased illegal distribution of the means of production and capital as well as widespread corruption.[63] Co-operators have attempted to defend themselves by insisting that they must resort to such activities in order to satisfy their production needs.[64] The press has assiduously chronicled these and other such activities within the co-operatives, and has even suggested co-operative links with the Soviet 'mafia'.

Reports of thefts and embezzlement in the co-operative sector are careful to note that these crimes are also a feature of the state sector; that false income tax returns, concealment of members' personal records, false information on types of production and false accounting are common, and invariably connected with the business of procuring supplies, is in the main put down to the pre-existing legal situation and frequent lack of control.[65] Other explanations ascribe any shortcomings to ignorance of the regulations and procedures. However, there can be no doubt that a combination of new opportunities and new needs has led to increased crime in the co-operatives, and also an association in the public mind between co-operatives and the 'mafia'.[66] Certainly, the vulnerability of the co-operatives and the common assumption that they possess large amounts of liquid assets, and are unwilling to account for them, have tended to attract the attention of organised crime.[67] It is a fact, though, that extortion is frequent and in the form of payments for 'protection'.

The measures taken by the police have ranged all the way from snap inspections and, more recently, to closures.[68] The co-operators, unhappy with such measures, complain bitterly of unjust accusations, lack of police protection, and prohibitions instead of support.[69]

CONSOLIDATION AND REGULATION

The first phase of co-operation, lasting from May 1987 to June 1988, was necessarily imperfect and insecure; the second phase, up to the spring of 1989, was a period of expansion following the passing of the Law on Co-operatives. This new-won security was characterised by conflicts with bureaucracy and growing disenchantment on the part of the public. All along the movement has been assuming a more organised form. The authorities have been concerned by the social tensions and the economic repercussions, while local bureaucracy has used every opportunity to further its own interests.

The issue of taxation led to sharp clashes from the very first. Attempts to introduce new taxes when the Law on Co-operatives was passed were halted by the unique procedure of remitting a proposal to the Commission on the Law, which promptly dropped it.[70] However, new laws were adopted in 1989, the purpose of which was not only to restrain co-operative incomes but also to stimulate a restructuring of the movement, differentiating between categories of co-operative according to regional criteria; branch, conditions of procuring supplies, social usefulness and categories of employees were also included. Taxation was related to the production year, with taxes remaining low the first year, raised the second year, and reaching a maximum the third year. The objectives of the law were stated to be to ensure social justice and to protect the interests of society.[71]

It is unclear whether a structure has been found which will ensure that such objectives will be attained or even approached. New elements of democracy and of administrative reform may turn out to be a restraining force. Although the bureaucracy would seem to have acquired a new weapon, the executive organs have been losing more and more of their power to the elected assemblies. Decisions on co-operative affairs are coming under the jurisdiction of commissions of People's Deputies. Thus, co-operative activity is increasingly being seen for what it is and for what it contributes, and is becoming less the object of popular prejudice.

The new tax regulations have brought income tax returns and centralised inspection.[72] Financial control is, in consequence, better managed and more legally based.[73] The benefit of such changes is that economic crime is stemmed, while the disadvantage is that local authorities are in a position to put a break on the development of co-operatives.

In December 1988 certain forms of health care, production of some medicines, films, video tapes and printed matter were first to come under prohibition, with production allowed only under the control of a *garant* (guarantor) in the form of a state institution, enterprise or organisation.[74] According to reports this regulation has been administered flexibly (or inefficiently!).[75] In October 1989 retail trade and mediating co-operatives were accused of speculation,[76] but after a stormy debate in the USSR Supreme Soviet attempts to impose new prohibitions were voted down. However, the aftertaste lingered. The trade unions backed up the criticisms,[77] and local authorities began to ban all kinds of co-operatives.[78] The First Secretary of Krasnodar *krai* (later the Russian party leader) likened co-operatives to '. . . a cancer, a social evil'.[79]

Not only did such slogans as 'Down with co-operatives!' figure usefully in elections, the bureaucracy was also able to gain in public sympathy.[80] A third prohibition wave began in February 1990, adding medical care and public catering to the list.[81] The distinction between national laws and local practice, which serves to damage co-operation and win popularity for some officials, places the national leadership in something of a dilemma. On the one hand, they do not want to risk the support of local bureaucracy, while on the other hand, their duty is to protect the legal rights and interests of co-operatives.[82]

Despite formidable resistance, co-operation is becoming more and more organised as a movement. The development of a network of contacts has helped in the procurement of supplies, with pooling of resources and other forms of mutual assistance.[83] However, members are wary of bureaucratism and excessive control by a centralised organisation, and it is a caution which appears to be well founded.[84]

To date, a number of regional and inter-regional co-operative unions have been created with minimal staffs and a very great degree of freedom for the members.[85] One of the more recent, formed in July 1989, has become the virtual spokesman of the movement in contacts with the authorities. It has also served to stimulate debate on the movement's principles, methods and goals, and to press for re-organisation where warranted. While the authorities have welcomed such debate, it has not found universal favour among co-operators.[86]

INTENTIONS AND EFFECTS OF REGULATION

The new tax regulations were intended not only to benefit the national economy; they were also aimed at obviating conflicts over disparities in incomes by inhibiting the growth of private fortunes, and facilitating the reorganisation of the co-operative structure through selective economic regulation. The (unfair) advantage of the co-operatives in the competition for the best labour was to be reduced, and the weakest links in the movement, so apt to generate the severest conflicts, were to be eliminated.

Whatever the beneficial effects of the latter measures for the national economy, they have reacted negatively upon the co-operatives and have even tended to subvert their very principles. Thus, any additional regulation can be interpreted as a regression to the command system, limiting the independence of the co-operatives and strengthening the grip of the bureaucracy. Even the orientation to the market is reduced thereby. All of this militates against the interests of the co-operators and makes the work less attractive. Indeed, the co-operators actually argue that any regulatory campaign will be taken advantage of by the 'enemy' (that is, the bureaucracy) in order to increase restrictions, an argument to which events have lent considerable substance.

At a meeting on 27 February 1990 the Moscow branch of the Co-operative Union, in near despair at the threat of yet another wave of prohibitions, proposed that the movement should be politicised even to the point of becoming a fully-fledged party. Towards this end a campaign of civil disobedience should be launched commencing with a refusal to submit income tax returns.

GOALS AND ACCOMPLISHMENTS

Judged on the statistics alone, the growth in the co-operative movement is impressive: in 1989 the number of participants, in excess of 5 million, was 3.5 times what it had been when the movement was first legalised; the number of registered co-operatives increased 2.5 times over the same period, reaching 193 400; the co-operative share of total Soviet GNP rose from 1 to 4.4 per cent, or approximately 40 billion roubles.[87] All the same, the numbers give an exaggerated impression of the strength of the movement, since 35 per cent of the workforce is part-time and some 40 per cent of workers are casually employed.[88] In addition, a number of co-operatives are severely indebted and under threat of closure.

Co-operation is entering a more stable period, helped in part by the present problem of scarcities of consumer goods and services, and construction materials. The co-operative share of sales of consumer goods is up to 9 per cent and is 15 per cent of consumer services.[89] Again, the strategic importance of co-operation owes much to its concentration in the large cities and in certain, for example Baltic, republics. Therefore, any unwarranted restrictions or prohibitions could seriously damage the economy of these regions.

The figures are remarkable given the frequent complaints about real and artificial obstacles put in the way of co-operative working. What is also astonishing is the fact that growth appears unbroken in spite of the reports of uncertainty about the future and the reliability of the actual policy. Nor do the new tax regulations appear to have had their feared effects. The reports and debates about impending disaster have so far been exaggerated.

Recent opinion polls on co-operation found that 50 per cent of the public are indifferent to it, one third of the remainder have a positive attitude to it and the other two thirds are negative.[90] V. Tikhonov, chairman of the Co-operative Union, states that about 70 per cent of people have no contact with co-operatives, and that most of the opponents of the movement are to be found among these; they are typically of the age group 55–60 years, and, he argues, have formed their opinions on the movement without having much knowledge or experience of it. However important, the latter is only one more argument in the debate.[91]

Nonetheless, the attractiveness of working in the co-operative sector was revealed by the fact that 31.2 per cent of those surveyed were willing to join a co-operative. Asked if they would want their children to join co-operatives, only 7.1 per cent answered in the affirmative, although a huge 68.2 per cent thought it a matter of choice. While the motive for joining was thought by 37.7 per cent to be expectation of high incomes, the other 62.3 per cent were attracted by the creative work and the desire to escape administrative pressure.[92] This might explain the unbroken growth in co-operation, even under difficult conditions, and suggest a readiness to accept reduced material rewards if security is guaranteed. The figures also indicate the existence of a reservoir of recruits in the event that conditions become easier.

The co-operatives were expected to contribute to the satisfaction of the country's economic and social needs in an acceptable form, and also to serve the process of reform. The rate of growth of the movement and the weight of public opinion are an important measurement of the results. However, the question that must be answered is how these goals have been achieved in qualitative terms.

The general goals were to increase production of goods and services, introduce elements of the market mechanism into the Soviet economy, reduce the administrative power of the bureaucracy, establish competition with the state monopoly, and give a legal and regulated status to activities conducted within the shadow economy. The principles were framed to take account of these goals, especially in respect of independence and market orientation. Internal democracy was to be both a principle and a general value; small-scale production was deemed a necessity and also a value in its own right.

The co-operative share of the production of goods and services is substantial, but several factors have reduced the value of its contribution. In the first place, property has been transferred from the state to the co-operatives, and some production removed from the illegal to the legal sector. In the second place, goods have been redistributed from the open, or state, supply network. While the advantages of the latter are disputed, it has brought additional quantities of production on to the market. Thirdly, the co-operatives have substantially increased purchasing power and demand, although it is questionable whether, in the final result, increased supplies will reach consumers in general.[93] Certainly, those with less purchasing power are losing out.

The market mechanism is limited in that co-operatives have been attached to state enterprises, supplies provided through state channels, and production determined by the system of *goszakazy* (state orders).[94] Total price regulation is decided locally,[95] and is demand-led. The choice of branches has been mainly the result of opportunities for filling practical needs and of expectations of profit. Lack of information on the demand structure, of market intelligence, of advertising or of exchange of experience is still typical.[96]

The principle of independence is considered a mockery by co-operators, as legal and financial controls and bureaucratic formalities often assume overwhelming proportions. It has been argued that co-operatives are subordinated to 'an endless number of "masters" consisting of executive committees, departments, ministries, social and control organizations, guarantors, law makers'.[97] Dependency relations are the consequence of active resistance on the part of bureaucracy, but they are also survivals from the past and functionally essential to the present stage of development of the market mechanism. Economic self-administration has resulted in high incomes and low rates of investment, which has excited public protest and ensured that the co-operative movement remains weak.

The goals of competition and legalisation of 'black' money have been no more successful. Competition with state production has, in practice, sometimes seen state monopoly become co-operative monopoly.[98] Where it has been established in fact, competition has taken on some negative aspects: it has led to industrial espionage,[99] has made little difference in respect of quality, and has had the unintended result of stimulating competition for labour, a constant source of conflict. Legalisation of part of the shadow economy has extended the regulated economy, but taxation and fees have limited expansion.[100] The frequency and variety of illegalities has increased, crime within the co-operatives is common and extends into the community, and there is now a firm link with organised crime.

Small-scale activity was preferred for the reason of easier access to supplies and to allow for greater capacity for expansion. The increased dimensions of the movement's activities have put a strain on the economic environment at large.[101] The small co-operatives, on the other hand, are those most criticised for their unscrupulous pricing policy and lack of concern for quality. The advantages of fast adaptation to demand is of little importance in determining the kinds of activities in which co-operatives engage in the face of the other considerations outlined above.

Internal democracy is rarely debated but is doubtless the object of frequent violations. However, the authorities, the public and the co-operators themselves appear untroubled by it, as attention is concentrated more on working and surviving. In any event, it is not in the interest of dissatisfied parties to raise such issues where there is still great competition for the few jobs; pressure from the authorities and the public has the effect of damping down internal conflict. In other circumstances, violation of democratic principles could turn out to be a problem both to the authorities and to the co-operators, in that democratic participation is an important value from the socialist and co-operative ideological perspectives. The lack of interest in the question in the Soviet debate tells us something of the present motives for participating in co-operative activity, and of the needs and expectations of politicians and the authorities.

These tendencies are the logical consequence of the introduction of market principles into the command structure. The disappointment and bitterness expressed by co-operators is understandable if less than realistic; it might also be counterproductive. Indeed, co-operators must work in accordance with economic demands and with the imprint of the past still on the system. Idealism will only be justified when there are changes in principles and circumstances.

The conclusion is that goals and principles have been distorted and the expected results have not been achieved. A balanced account of the positive and negative effects requires complex calculations of the co-operative impact on supply and demand for consumer goods and the effects on the shadow economy. It requires, moreover, an analysis of the impact upon attitudes to principles, and relations between groups of actors involved in co-operative activities. Here we have only been able to look at the problem in bare outline.

The goals and principles have not, as such, been revised, therefore any failure is relative and final conclusions cannot be drawn. Commitment on the part of the political leadership remains strong. In addition, co-operation fills important needs in production and services, it

shows itself highly productive, and it gives opportunities for independent and creative work. It also serves as yet another link in the
transition to a market economy and the struggle against the
bureaucracy. Its symbolic significance is high also through its association with the early days of Soviet power and as another form of social
property. Even if a high price must be paid today in loss of prestige
and political support, the leadership is unlikely to impose wide-
ranging prohibitions.

THE FUTURE OF COOPERATION

Co-operation has not yielded the expected results, nor have the goals
which were set been achieved. There has been frequent and systema-
tic violation of principles. The economic and social effects have
neither advanced an alternative socialist model, as was originally
intended, nor raised the esteem of market mechanisms in the eyes of
the public. The bureaucracy has been challenged but not forced back.
Many co-operators have distanced themselves from both the present
government and from *perestroika*. The question we must now ask is
whether co-operation has a future.

Several scenarios are discernible, but I shall limit myself to two that
are 'realistic'. The first of these is that of a cautious and gradual
introduction of market relations. As was noted above, the political
and administrative changes have to some degree transformed the
conditions for co-operative activity, possibly in favour of the promotion of co-operative interests. One precondition is, however, that the
movement itself continues to organise along the lines of self-help and
conforms to new local processes. The new liberal parties support
co-operation in principle but they cannot afford a movement which
evokes the kinds of antagonisms and social phenomena which have so
far been the co-operative reality. Given such a perspective, the
further development of co-operation will continue in more organised
forms, assuming a more democratic internal structure and adapting
slowly to customer expectations and demands. It would then correspond to the original model but now in a democratic environment and
with stronger emphasis upon a fully-fledged market mechanism. One
might well assume a more optimistic prospect with the adoption of
political pluralism and on-going administrative reform.

The second scenario would suggest a more rapid transformation
with unlimited forms of ownership and full market relations within a

couple of years. Such a perspective would probably allow the co-operatives to develop rapidly in the next few years, with the continuation of some of the present negative traits and also sharp social conflicts with the public. The current conflict, which is centred on inputs, would be resolved by the introduction of a market trade in all supplies. Price spirals and inflation would assume new proportions. Thus, a system approximating to classic capitalism is envisaged which would lead to the speedy privatisation of the most successful co-operatives now benefiting from a rapid accumulation of individual capital. There is neither a strong socialist nor a strong co-operative ideology to motivate adherence to present property relations. It is, furthermore, the common experience that workers' co-operatives can survive in a capitalist environment only under special conditions. On the other hand, a process may have been started that will lead to the formation of a new movement based upon a more genuine co-operative ideology, whose members will have a social background and associated needs more typical of those that exist in the West.

Notes

1. See *Materialy XXVII s"ezda KPSS* (Moscow: Politizdat, 1986) pp. 39 and 59. The main decision was taken at the Central Committee plenum in January 1987. See *Kommunist*, 1987, no. 3, p. 8.
2. See *Ekonomicheskaya gazeta*, 1987, no. 9.
3. See *Zakon Soyuza Sovetskikh Sotsialisticheskikh Respublik o kooperatsii v SSSR* (Moscow: Izvestiya, 1988).
4. See ibid. See also, for example, N. I. Ryzhkov, 'O roli kooperatsii v razvitii ekonomiki strany i proekte zakona o kooperatsii v SSSR', in *Kooperatsiya i arenda*, vol. 1 (Moscow: Politizdat, 1989) pp. 113–62; *Pravda*, 20 March 1988; and *Trud*, 19 April 1988.
5. See previous note. See also M. S. Gorbachev, *Potentsial kooperatsii-delu perestroiki* (Moscow: IPL, 1988); P. Savchenko and P. Mar'ianovsky, 'Kooperativnaya sobstvennost' pri sotsializme: vozmozhnosti i perspektivy', *Planovoe khozyaistvo*, 1988, no. 2, pp. 112–16; and A. Ya. Maksimovich, 'Stanovlenie i razvitie novykh kooperativov', *Sovetskoe gosudarstvo i pravo*, 1988, no. 2, pp. 22–9.
6. See Boris Kurashvili in *Moskovskie novosti*, 1989, no. 12.
7. See, for example, *Sotsialisticheskaya industriya*, 21 April and 24 March 1989; *Izvestiya*, 24 October 1988.
8. See ibid., 23 November 1988 and 18 January 1989.
9. These rules were criticised and frequently broken. See A. Arkhipov, T. Kuznetsova, 'Novye formy kooperatsii: pervye itogi i problemy',

Voprosy ekonomiki, 1987, no. 11, pp. 142–55.
10. See Gorbachev, *Potentsial*, and N. Golovnin, M. Krans, V. Nekhotin, 'Vremya initsiativnykh lyudei', *Kommunist*, 1989, no. 1, pp. 21–35; also A. Livshits, 'Kooperativnyi sektor: problemy gosudarstvennogo regulirovaniya', *Planovoe khozyaistvo*, 1990, no. 1, pp. 104–9.
11. See, for example, *Izvestiya*, 6 March 1989; *Moskovskie novosti*, 1989, no. 12; *Literaturnaya gazeta*, 20 July 1988.
12. See comments on the general state of the law in *Moskovskie novosti*, 1988, no. 47; and *Izvestiya*, 24 November 1989. See also V. Selyunin, 'Chernye dyry ekonomiki', *Novyi mir*, 1989, no. 10, pp. 153–78.
13. See the poll in *Sotsialisticheskaya industriya*, 24 March 1989.
14. See Livshits, 'Kooperativnyi sektor'.
15. Criticism is common of passivity and incompetence; see *Sotsialisticheskaya industriya*, 18 January 1989.
16. See, for examples of the cooperative position, 'Vo vlasti stikhii', *Khozyaistvo i pravo*, 1989, no. 11, pp. 43–51.
17. Spare parts from wrecked machinery have been reported not accessible for unclear reasons.
18. To include a bureaucrat among the members has been ironically noted as a solution to many problems. See, for examples of bribery and other illegalities, *Moskovski novosti*, 1988, no. 51, and 1989, no. 5; *Literaturnaya gazeta*, 17 August 1988 and 11 January 1989; and *Sovetskaya Rossiya*, 17 September 1988.
19. See *Ekonomika i zhizn'*, 1990, nos. 1 and 3.
20. See, for example, *Sovetskaya Rossiya*, 11 October 1989.
21. See *Moskovskie novosti*, 1988, no. 43. In *Sotsialisticheskaya industriya*, 21 December 1988, cooperatives are said to have the right to buy 43 per cent of supplies in state shops.
22. Auctions have become one form. See *Moskovskie novosti*, 1988, no. 45. In Leningrad 80 per cent of public catering is co-operative; in Moscow the share is 60 per cent: see *Pravda*, 5 October 1989. Illegal sale of high technology is reported in *Sovetskaya Rossiya*, 27 September 1989.
23. See N. Shmelev, 'Libo sila, libo rubl'', *Znamya*, 1989, no. 1, p. 132. See also A. Ivanchenko, N. Postovoi, 'Kooperatsia: nachalo puti', *Sovety narodnykh deputatov*, 1988, no. 12, pp. 28–34.
24. See *Sotsialisticheskaya industriya*, 21 December 1988 ('Schet vedet "shchegol"').
25. See V. Pisigin in *Sotsialisticheskaya industriya*, 18 January 1988 ('Argumenty za arendu').
26. See *Sovetskaya Rossiya*, 25 February 1990.
27. See, for example, *Ekonomicheskaya gazeta*, 1987, nos. 24 and 39.
28. See, for example *Izvestiya*, 27 February 1988 and 12 October 1989.
29. See, for cases of such refusals, A. Arkhipov, T. Kuznetsova, 'Novye formy kooperatsii: pervye itogi i problemy', *Voprosy ekonomiki*, 1987, no. 11, pp. 142–55; *Sotsialisticheskaya industriya*, 21 December 1988 ('Glavnoe-proyavit' tverdost'') and 12 December 1988 ('Opekun ili sopernik'); *Sovetskaya Rossiya*, 7 August 1987 and 21 February 1988.
30. See *Moskovskie novosti*, 1989, no. 39.

31. According to the law co-operative taxes go directly to the local budget.
32. *Izvestiya*, 3 February 1990.
33. *Izvestiya*, 11 February 1990.
34. See, for example, *Sotsialisticheskaya industriya*, 21 December 1988.
35. *Izvestiya*, 11 February 1990.
36. The agreements have often been changed in an unpermitted way, but the co-operative has had to accept. See, for example, *Izvestiya*, 24 October 1988, and *Sotsialisticheskaya industriya*, 29 September 1989 ('Po zakonam konkurentsii').
37. Such advantages have been critically observed. The negative effect may be that low productivity in the state sector is perpetuated. Compare Savchenko and Mar'ianovsky, 'Kooperativnaya sobstvennost'', p. 115.
38. Demands are exemplified in *Moskovskie novosti*, 1989, no. 16.
39. See *Centrosoyuz Review*, 1990, no. 6, p. 27.
40. Competition of labour concerns also the state authorities, aš recruitment is extended into other local sectors of the economy. See *Sovetskaya Rossiya*, 30 July 1989.
41. Contracted part-time workers have constituted almost half the number of participants but the share is slowly decreasing. It is now between 35 and 40 per cent. See *Moskovskie novosti*, 1990, no. 12.
42. See the report in *Sotsialisticheskaya industriya*, 29 September 1989 ('Opekun ili sopernik'). See also ibid., 27 October 1989 ('Stroka iz doklada').
43. See, for example, *Sotsialisticheskaya industriya*, 23 November 1988 ('Garant otreksya').
44. See *Ekonomika i zhizn'*, 1990, no. 16 ('Uravnyat' ekonomicheskie usloviya').
45. This is one of the most criticised factors in co-operative policy. See, for example, *Ekonomicheskaya gazeta*, 1989, no. 13, and *Sovetskaya Rossiya*, 12 July 1989.
46. See, for example, Golovnin *et al.*, 'Vremya', pp. 22ff.
47. See the attacks on co-operation from the trade unions. *Trud*, 9 September 1989 and 23 January 1990.
48. The social distinction is clear but not dramatic. Co-operation is lowest in popularity among pensioners, peasants or agricultural workers, and workers, with percentages from 9.2 to 14.2, and highest among specialists and managers with a 'positive' rating of 22–25 per cent. See *Ekonomika i zhizn'*, 1990, no. 16.
49. In *Ekonomika i zhizn'*, 1990, no. 17, these two points are elaborated. Criticism is especially devoted to appropriation of surplus value from hired labour. *See also Argumenty i fakty*, 1990, no. 4.
50. New co-operation has been criticised for reinstating capitalism by The Association of Scientific Communism and The United Front of Working People.
51. See, for example, *Ekonomicheskaya gazeta*, 1988, no. 16 and *Literaturnaya gazeta*, 11 January 1989.
52. For further examples, see *Ekonomika i zhizn'*, 1990, nos. 1 and 3.
53. See *Moskovskie novosti*, 1990, no. 12 ('Beg s bar"erami').

54. See Selyunin, 'Chernye dyry ekonomiki' and also *Izvestiya*, 24 September 1989.
55. See *Moskovskie novosti*, 1988, no. 47 and 1989, no. 21, with two polemical articles by N. Shmelev.
56. See *Sovetskaya Rossiya*, 25 February 1990.
57. See *Sovetskaya Rossiya*, 30 July 1989 and *Izvestiya*, 26 October 1989.
58. See L. V. Babayeva, 'Kooperativy v zerkale obshchestvennogo mneniya', *EKO*, no. 2, pp. 89–96.
59. A recent poll shows that 20 per cent of the respondents consider that co-operation destroys socialism. See T. V. Avdeenko, V. A. Lisov, V. M. Rutgaizer, S. P. Shpil'ko, 'Novaya sovetskaya kooperatsia i naselenie', *Izvestiya sibirskogo otdeleniya Akademii nauk SSSR: ekonomika i sotsiologiya*, 1990, no. 1, pp. 15–19.
60. Fear of joining co-operatives for social reasons is sometimes expressed. See *Moskovskie novosti*, 1988, no. 43.
61. These risks are well-known in areas of strong mafia influence.
62. S. Golovnin and A. Shokhin report several estimations of the shadow economy. The capital is, according to the highest figures, 500 mrd roubles at the end of 1989. See *Kommunist*, 1990, no. 1, p. 51. T. Koryagina estimates that the turnover of the shadow economy has risen from 5 mrd roubles at the beginning of the 1960s to 90 mrd roubles at the end of the 1980s, and further to about 100 mrd roubles in 1990. It is also reported that the detected economic crimes in 1989 amounted to 257 000. This is estimated to constitute 1 per cent of all these crimes. See Yu. Kozlov, 'Tenevaya ekonomika i prestupnost'', *Voprosy ekonomiki*, 1990, no. 3, pp. 120–7.
63. See, for example, *Ekonomika i zhizn'*, 1990, no. 3, pp. 120–7.
64. An investigation indicates that 80–85 per cent of all co-operatives systematically violate legal rules. *Voprosy ekonomiki*, 1990, no. 3, p. 123.
65. The sum of revealed embezzlements in co-operatives were in 1989 150 million roubles. Ibid., p. 124.
66. Many crimes within the co-operation are connected to organised crime; the connection is not only pressed upon co-operation, it also emanates from within the movement. See ibid.
67. This is exemplified in *Literaturnaya gazeta*, 17 January 1990.
68. See, for example, *Izvestiya*, 12 October 1989 and *Moskovskie novosti*, 1989, no. 13.
69. See, for example, *Moskovskie novosti*, 1989, no. 41, *Izvestiya*, 25 October 1989 and *Izvestiya*, 2 February 1990.
70. See I. Yefremov, 'Progress or progression?', *New Times*, 1988, no. 34, pp. 28–31, and J. Tedstrom, 'Soviet co-operatives: a difficult road to legitimacy', *Radio Liberty Research*, 31 May 1988.
71. See *Ekonomicheskaya gazeta*, 1989, nos. 15 and 37, and *Izvestiya*, 9 August 1989.
72. Tax inspections have been created at the Ministry of Finance. People's control is expected to support their work. Co-operative spokesmen have criticised the decision. See *Sotsialisticheskaya industriya*, 21 April 1989.

73. See *Izvestiya*, 25 October 1989. *Izvestiya*, 12 October 1989 carries information on new legal measures.
74. See *Izvestiya*, 31 December 1988.
75. The problem of finding a guarantor is a minor one. A consequence which is worse is that the system is sometimes integrated into the bribery system.
76. See, for example, N. Solyanik, 'Kooperatsiya: ostrye diskussii', *Sovety narodnykh deputatov*, 1989, no. 11, pp. 6–8, and *Centrosoyuz Review*, September–October 1989.
77. The demand for prohibition was raised already by striking miners in the summer of 1989. See, for example, *Sotsialisticheskaya industriya*, 29 September 1989 ('Ot redaktsii').
78. See *Sotsialisticheskaya industriya*, 29 September 1989 ('Derzhat' i ne pushchat'!').
79. See *Izvestiya*, 11 February 1990.
80. See *Moskovskie novosti*, 1989, no. 39 and *Izvestiya*, 11 February 1990.
81. See *Komsomol'skaya pravda*, 20 February 1990.
82. The discussion in *Moskovskie novosti*, 1990, no. 6, between representatives of high authorities and co-operators is illustrative.
83. See Golovnin et al., 'Vremya', p. 22.
84. See, for example, *Sotsialisticheskaya industriya*, 23 November 1988 and *Literaturnaya gazeta*, 20 July 1988.
85. Practical work has been stated to be marginal and the organisations are soon forgotten. See *Sotsialisticheskaya industriya*, 29 September 1989.
86. The new co-operative union has been cautiously criticised for solving problems in contact with the state organs. See *Moskovskie novosti*, 1990, no. 12, and *Sotsialisticheskaya industriya*, 29 September 1989.
87. See *Ekonomika i zhizn'*, 1990, no. 12.
88. Ibid.
89. Ibid.
90. See *Sovetskaya Rossiya*, 25 October 1989.
91. *EKO*, 1990, no. 4, p. 4.
92. *Sovetskaya Rossiya*, 25 October 1989.
93. See *Ekonomika i zhizn'*, 1990, no. 5, p. 18.
94. Goskomstat reports that 80 per cent of all co-operatives are connected to state enterprises or organisations. They rent 60 per cent of basic funds, get 60 per cent of their raw material and sell about 70 per cent of production and service to state enterprises. *Ekonomika i zhizn'*, 1990, no. 12, p. 5. V. A. Tikhonov reports in *EKO*, 1990, no. 4, pp. 12f, that production co-operatives working on state requests are about 37 per cent.
95. The amendments to the co-operative law in October 1989 stipulated several price restrictions, including the right of local price regulation. See *Sovetskaya Rossiya*, 21 October 1989.
96. See, for example, *Sotsialisticheskaya industriya*, 23 November 1988, and *Literaturnaya gazeta*, 11 January 1989.
97. *Khozyaistvo i pravo*, 1990, no. 3, p. 65.
98. See, for one example, *Literaturnaya gazeta*, 11 January 1989.
99. *Voprosy ekonomiki*, 1990, no. 3, p. 124.

100. See *Izvestiya*, 27 October 1989.
101. Small-scale production is, however, dominant. The average number is 25 participants. The largest co-operatives are found in the sector of building with 1 516 500 participants in 38 700 co-operatives, that is, an average number of 40. See *Moskovskie novosti*, 1990, no. 12.

3 Drug Abuse in the USSR
John M. Kramer

> Until recently, we in the Soviet Union were firmly convinced that drug addiction was a problem only in other countries. There never had been or ever could be any social grounds for addiction here. But facts are facts: the number of our people who suffer from this terrible ailment is growing.
>
> *Bakinskii rabochii*, 26 August 1986

Only since Mikhail Gorbachev came to power in 1985 has the USSR acknowledged the existence of a real and growing problem with drug abuse.[1] As late as the mid 1980s, commentaries claimed that in the Soviet Union 'serious drug addiction does not exist', 'no minors suffer from drug addiction', 'not a single case' of addiction to amphetamines, cocaine, heroin, and LSD had been recorded, and there was even a 'tendency towards a decline' in the limited extant addiction. The few individuals who had become addicts (officially estimated in 1985 at between 2500 and 3000 persons) mostly did so unwittingly while being treated for chronic diseases.[2] However, available evidence belies these claims.

There was widespread use of addictive drugs during World War I among Russian soldiers, in the revolution that toppled Tsardom, and in the first decade of Soviet power.[3] Reportedly, a 'narco mafia' operated in World War I, supplying Russian soldiers with cocaine and other addictive drugs. Bolsheviks during the revolution often used drugs to 'fight tiredness and reduce tension'. At the height of the revolution, 'Clubs of Morphinists' were uncovered among naval personnel who regularly bought and sold drugs. The dearth of medicines during these years made the use of morphine and opium as painkillers commonplace.

The authorities enacted several legal measures to combat this behaviour.[4] In 1926, the Criminal Code of the RSFSR established criminal responsibility for the 'production and storage of cocaine, morphine, and other narcotic substances for sale without proper authorisation' and for maintaining premises where narcotics were used or sold. In 1928, the USSR prohibited the free circulation of cocaine, its salts, hashish, opium, morphine, heroin, and other narcotic substances. These initiatives were taken to combat 'an outbreak of narcomania' in the 1920s.

Several initiatives in the 1930s also sought this end. In 1934, a joint decree of the All-Union Central Executive Committee and the USSR Council of People's Commissars prohibited sowing opium poppies and Indian hemp, except in legally designated areas, on territory of the USSR. Thereupon, the Criminal Code of the RSFSR established criminal responsibility for these acts. The USSR Council of Ministers issued a decree in 1935 'charging the All-Union Inspectorate of the USSR Council of People's Commissars with Observing and Overseeing the Circulation of Opium and Other Narcotic Substances'.

The next legal initiatives against drug abuse appeared in the 1960s. In 1966, the USSR Supreme Court and its counterpart in the Russian Republic convened plenary sessions that examined, *inter alia*, legal issues involved in the prosecution of individuals accused of manufacturing and distributing 'narcotics, harsh acting substances, and poisons'.[5] Reports of a 'large number of drug users' in the military, particularly among soldiers serving in Central Asia, seemingly prompted their concern.[6]

In 1972, the Principles of Criminal Legislation of the USSR and the Union Republics added under 'grave crimes' the 'theft, manufacture, acquisition, or possession of narcotics for the purpose of sale, and/or the sale of such substances'. The Russian Republic in the same year decreed that narcotics addicts were subject to 'compulsory treatment and labour re-education' in medical and labour therapy institutions for terms of one to two years.[7] Then, in 1974, the USSR Supreme Soviet issued a decree, 'On Intensifying the Struggle Against Drug Addiction', that specified many measures to combat this phenomenon.[8] Finally, in 1975 the USSR Supreme Court again examined the issue of drug addiction. It did so 'not because the scale of drug addiction has became menacing in any way, but because . . . this poison must be killed in its infancy'.[9]

Officials in the republic of Georgia appeared more concerned about drug abuse than their peers in other republics. As early as 1967, they wondered:

Why were hemp and poppies being grown in areas of Georgia where they had not been sown in the past? Why were many young people with no ties to the criminal world and no previous convictions turning up among drug addicts? Why were there a growing number of crimes – thefts, speculation, extortion – committed for a single purpose: to obtain money immediately?[10]

In 1967, the republic's Ministry of Internal Affairs (MVD) and the Komsomol established a special commission to study the problem. Professor Anzor Gabiani (now among the most prominent drug specialists in the former USSR) completed extensive primary research on drug abuse in Georgia in the 1960s and 1970s for a classified audience.[11] Gabiani also reported that a 'narco mafia' with a 'well organised and ramified structure' controlled the trade in illicit drugs. Perhaps in retaliation for this revelation, Gabiani's flat was set on fire, his life threatened, and pressure successfully exerted to close his laboratory.[12] One of his studies, whose findings were published only in 1987, found, *inter alia*, that among its sample the consumption of opium-based derivatives occupied 'first place' – thereby refuting official claims that consumption of such drugs was still 'practically unheard of' in the USSR.[13]

The ascension to power of Mikhail Gorbachev as General Secretary of the Communist Party initiated a dramatic change in the official attitude towards drug abuse. Reflecting the General Secretary's campaign for *glasnost'* and for delving into social pathologies, the official media have carried numerous revealing accounts – frequently employing lurid, even hyperbolic language – portraying a much wider incidence of what Soviet sources themselves often label 'narcomania'. In the words of one contemporary:

> Concealing an illness will not make it go away; it will only drive it inward. We have come to realize that openness is needed in the struggle against drug addiction; that we must look truth in the eye, no matter how unsavory that is.[14]

SCOPE OF THE PROBLEM

It is difficult to gauge the actual dimensions of drug abuse in the USSR.[15] Western states encounter a similar problem. For example, an official with the United States Institute of Drug Abuse asserts that 'you just can't trust the numbers' when assessing drug abuse in American society.[16]

Several factors create this imprecision. First, terms such as 'abuse', 'addiction', 'dependency', and 'misuse' have no universally accepted

definitions and often are employed interchangeably.[17] Soviet sources
frequently exhibit this imprecision by referring to all drugs – regardless of their pharmacological properties – as 'narcotics' and all users
as 'addicts'. Reportedly, Soviet researchers classify a substance as
'narcotic' if it has a 'specific effect' (stimulation, sedation, hallucina-
tion, and so on) on the central nervous system and its usage has
attained 'social significance'.[18] Such sweeping criteria permit labelling
as 'narcotic' many substances that would not commonly be considered so in the United States.[19]

According to E. A. Babayan, Chairman of the Standing Committee
on the Control of Narcotics of the USSR Ministry of Health – the
principal co-ordinating body charged with controlling production and
use of narcotic and psychotropic substances in the USSR – the term
'narcomania' describes a 'state induced by the use of narcotic substances' and is employed when 'non-medical use occurs of a substance
which by law is classified as a narcotic substance'. In contrast, the
term 'toxicomania' 'defines the damage to health' which is induced by
the non-medical use of a substance 'which has not yet been juridically
recognised as being narcotic'.[20] Unfortunately, these terms themselves exhibit terminological imprecision. For example, how precisely
does one define – and what criteria are employed to measure – that
'state' which narcomania induces or that 'damage to health' which
toxicomania describes? It is a truism, however, that no completely
satisfactory term exists to describe the behaviour we denote with
'drug abuse'. Consequently, the present study employs the term 'drug
abuse' while recognising the ambiguity inherent in its use.

Second, drug abusers in all societies often seek for both personal
and professional reasons to conceal their condition. They especially
do so in the USSR where even casual drug users are registered with
the police and often subject to severe legal penalties. Society often
exhibits little sympathy for drug abusers. Enterprises fire such people
'left and right' thereby making them social 'outcasts', one official
reports.[21]

Third, only since 1988 has the USSR published even incomplete
data on the extent of drug and toxin addiction nationally and in the
union republics (see Table 3.1). Further, the dictates of *glasnost'*
notwithstanding, Soviet officials appear ambivalent about how candidly they should discuss this issue:

We know little about the social reverberations that the published
materials will have, about the influence they will have on different

Table 3.1 Individuals registered at medical institutions with a diagnosis of narcomania and toxicomania
(per 100 000 of population)

	1980	*1985*	*1987*	*1988*
USSR	13.6	14.9	21.5	24.3
Union Republics				
Armenia			6.3	6.5
Azerbaidzhan			11.1	14.1
Belorussia			4.8	5.9
Estonia			10.3	14.0
Georgia			17.7	19.2
Kazakhstan			26.5	30.9
Kirgizia			29.0	26.7
Latvia			19.0	22.6
Lithuania			10.1	11.2
Moldavia			8.0	8.3
Russia			17.9	20.6
Tajikistan			9.1	10.5
Turkmenistan			129.9	109.8
Ukraine			32.4	37.4
Uzbekistan			20.8	24.2

Sources: For 1980 *Narodnoe khozyaistvo SSSR v 1987 g.* (Moscow: Finansy i statistika, 1988) p. 549. For 1985–8 *Sotsial'noe razvitie SSSR* (Moscow: Goskomstat, 1990) p. 269.

groups of the population, particularly on youth. The possibility is not excluded that the publication of materials in the press with elements of sensationalism may generate an interest in narcotics, may inspire the search for them, etc.[22]

However, the available materials on drug abuse do permit several generalisations. First, official statistics about drug abuse – which include only those individuals registered with the police and medical institutions – substantially understate the extent of the phenomenon. Thus, a ranking official in the USSR MVD recently admitted that registered addicts are a 'drop in the bucket' of all addicts whose number is 'truly huge'.[23] However, drug abuse is unlikely in the foreseeable future to supersede alcoholism as the pre-eminent social pathology in the Soviet Union. Second, the socio-economic charac-teristics of many drug abusers refute the often-articulated official image of them as socially maladjusted and 'parasitic' individuals incapable of gainful employment. The most comprehensive survey to date of drug abuse in the USSR, supervised by Professor Gabiani under the auspices of the USSR MVD, found that among individuals identified as 'drug addicts' approximately 85 per cent are employed, 70 per cent of those with jobs are workers (*rabochie*) while only 8 per cent are white-collar staff (*sluzhashchie*), and 75 per cent of them have at least a secondary education.[24] These data also differ from the findings of an earlier western study, that identified drug abuse as a phenomenon restricted primarily to the progeny of the middle and upper classes.[25]

Third, drug abusers acquire and consume drugs in ways similar (although not identical) to those in the West. They acquire drugs, *inter alia*, by stealing them, by producing them themselves, and by purchasing them illegally from drug dealers and often legally from pharmacies and other medical institutions. To support their habit, they engage in sundry illegalities ranging from prostitution to armed robbery. Users sniff glue, swallow amphetamines, barbiturates, and cough syrups with a high codeine content, smoke marijuana and hashish, inject themselves with heroin and consume other drugs in ways common to the drug scene in the West. In contrast, the consumption of narcotic drugs appears far less prevalent in the Soviet Union than in many Western states.[26] Fourth, young people predominate among drug users. The aforementioned study on drug abuse for the USSR MVD found that approximately 70 per cent of the individuals it identified as addicts and users were under the age of 30 and over 60 per cent of these individuals began using drugs before the age of 19.[27]

In 1990, 'around' 130 000 individuals were officially registered with the police for engaging in the 'non-medical use of drugs'. 'Over' 60 000 of these individuals 'suffer from drug addiction'.[28]

Table 1 provides data on individuals registered at medical institutions with a diagnosis of drug or toxin addiction. These data indicate that in 1988, compared to 1987 and 1980, the number of such individuals per 100 000 population in the USSR increased by approximately 11 and 36 per cent, respectively. In 1988, Turkmenistan possessed the dubious distinction of having (by far) the highest such index among the union republics. This index also exceeded the national average in Ukraine, Kirgizia, Kazakhstan and approximated it in Uzbekistan. In contrast, this index was at least one-half lower than the national average in the Armenian, Belorussian, Lithuanian, Moldavian, and Tajik SSRs.

These data must be assessed cautiously. First, they only indicate the number of addicts registered with medical institutions, not the number of addicts in the USSR. As noted, the latter figure undoubtedly far exceeds the former figure. Based on his research, Professor Gabiani calculates that the actual number of drug users and addicts exceeds the respective official figure by 10 to 12 times.[29] The chief of the USSR MVD Main Criminal Investigation Administration endorses this calculation.[30] Gabiani's calculation suggests that there are roughly 1.3–1.6 million drug users in the former USSR, including 600 000–720 000 drug addicts.

Second, Soviet officials provide vague and even incorrect definitions of what constitutes an 'addict', 'user', and a 'narcotic'. A ranking official in the USSR MVD reports that registered addicts are 'people whom doctors officially consider sick'. Users are individuals who consume 'narcotics' in 'one way or another or have already tried them . . . but whom doctors do not consider sick'. Hashish is the principal 'narcotic' consumed by a 'majority' of individuals in both categories.[31]

Such materials are of limited utility. They do not indicate what criteria doctors employ to determine how and when a person is sufficiently 'sick' to merit the appellation 'addict'. Similarly, a category that includes individuals who 'use' narcotics 'in one way or another or have already tried them' reveals little about the actual incidence of drug abuse. Finally, to consider hashish – which produces no physical and, usually, no psychological dependence – as a 'narcotic' is, at best, a debateable proposition.[32] To make no distinction between hashish and narcotic substances (for example, opiates) which produce both physical and psychological dependence is inaccurate.

Third, the number of 'addicts' registered at medical institutions may reveal more about the performance of officials in registering and reporting these individuals than it does about the actual incidence of drug abuse. For example, one can hypothesise that drug abuse is a serious problem in Moldavia since the Presidium of the USSR Supreme Soviet in 1988 heard a report on this subject.[33] Yet Table 3.1 indicates that in both 1987 and 1988 Moldavia had the third lowest number of registered addicts per 100 000 population of any union republic. This same index is also below the national average in the Caucasian republics of Armenia, Azerbaidzhan, and Georgia – but the chief of the USSR MVD Main Criminal Investigation Administration recently singled out the Caucasus as a region where drug addiction had become 'particularly widespread'.[34] Similarly, one suspects that the extremely low figure for registered addicts in Tajikistan in comparison to other Central Asian republics presents a misleading picture of the extent of drug abuse there. Other officials may seek to demonstrate their zeal in the fight against drugs by inflating the number of registered addicts in their republics. Turkmenistan, with its disproportionately higher number of registered addicts than the national average, may exhibit this circumstance. Such behaviour would parallel that displayed by officials in other 'campaigns' against social pathologies and deviant lifestyles.[35]

Research conducted by Professor Gabiani in the republic of Georgia provides data on the socio-economic background and drug-related activities of known drug users.[36] This research indicates that drug users were increasingly more likely than their earlier counterparts to be female, younger, better educated, affluent, and raised in families with both parents present. Finally, his research provides data on the usage of drugs. Individuals in the 1960s typically began to use drugs while in prison. In contrast, in later years users were far more likely to have become acquainted with drugs from friends and acquaintances at home and at school. This circumstance suggests that illicit drug use subsequently may have spread to a broader segment of the general population than was the case in the 1960s. The incidence of drug use differed little over time. Over 80 per cent of the individuals in his sundry samples consumed drugs at least once a day and a majority of them did so at least twice a day. However, a significant difference did emerge in the types of drugs that users consumed. Opiates occupied 'first place' among drugs consumed in the 1960s, while subsequently hashish held this status (although opiates continued to be among the 'most consumed' of narcotic substances).

Unfortunately, the absence of comparable national statistics prevents an assessment of how representative are these samples of drug users throughout the former Soviet Union (or even in Georgia itself). In turn, this circumstance reflects the impossibility of making definitive generalisations about the overall dimensions of drug abuse in the republics that formerly constituted the USSR.

THE CAUSES

There exists no definitive explanation for drug abuse. Western specialists advance a variety of (at times, conflicting) physiological, psychological, and socio-cultural hypotheses to explain this phenomenon.[37] Belated official *glasnost'*, in even acknowledging its existence, compounded the difficulty of developing an etiology of drug abuse in the USSR. Most commonly, Soviet commentaries identify a cluster of personal factors – boredom, curiosity, escapism, hedonism, the desire for acceptance by one's peers – motivating resort to drugs.[38]

In the opinion of a senior official in the USSR MVD, youths take drugs primarily out of curiosity aroused by sensationalist publications and 'idle' conversations among their peers on this subject.[39] In particular, many Soviet youths seek to emulate the hedonistic lifestyles, including the use of drugs, they allegedly encounter in foreign films and personal contacts with Westerners. Approximately 50 per cent of the drug addicts interviewed in one survey claimed they began their habit to emulate the 'beautiful life' of bourgeois society.[40] Reportedly, many individuals turn to drugs to escape from the trials and travails of their daily lives. 'Shortcomings' in the family often promote this circumstance. Broken homes, excessive drinking by parents, the absence of warm and loving bonds among family members are all seen as driving youths to seek solace in drugs.[41] Contrarily, drug abusers may have overly indulgent parents who spoil them and fail to discipline them appropriately. Such parents should face 'juridical responsibility' for actively or implicitly supporting the 'parasitic lifestyle' of their drug abusing progeny, one source contends.[42] Then too, drug abuse among certain ethnic groups (particularly Muslim peoples of Central Asia) supposedly represents a 'vestige of the past' where the consumption of drugs is embedded in the traditional culture. Reportedly, a 'fairly widespread phenomenon' in Turkmenistan involves giving babies tea with opium dissolved in it to calm them and induce sleep. It is not 'uncommon' for babies to die of narcotic overdoses from this practice.[43]

At times official policy is said, albeit unintentionally, to promote drug abuse. Thus, official reticence about drug abuse supposedly increases resort to drugs, because many drug users are unaware until it is too late of the pernicious physical and mental consequences of their actions. Calling for a comprehensive campaign to alert the citizenry to the dangers of drugs, a prominent drug treatment specialist contends that the public must understand that to use an illicit drug even once 'can lead to tragedy'.[44]

Other sources argue – without providing compelling evidence in substantiation – that Mikhail Gorbachev's campaign to combat alcoholism unintentionally fostered drug use among individuals who sought substitutes to satisfy their craving for vodka.[45] Soviet policy in Afghanistan may unwittingly have had similar consequences. Published accounts report widespread use of hashish and sundry opiates among Soviet troops in that country. Reportedly, upon their return to the Soviet Union many of these veterans continued their drug habit in part to erase memories of the war.[46] A senior coach of the USSR Track and Field Team recently revealed that the enormous pressure to succeed in international athletic competitions, especially the Olympics, sometimes leads participating athletes to abuse anabolic steroids and other performance-enhancing drugs. Soviet officials punished nearly 300 athletes for using banned substances in the three years preceding the 1988 Olympic Games.[47] Occasionally, official policy may even intentionally promote drug abuse. An exposé in *Ogonek*, a liberal periodical, charges that prison officials in Stavropol turned inmates into addicts by providing them with drugs. Officials exploited the ensuing dependence to extort confessions from the inmates and use them as informers against other prisoners.[48] Official policies have even been indicted for creating 'moral losses' and a 'moral vacuum' that promote drug abuse:

> If one thinks that upbringing is only a task of schools, family, slogans, and brilliant lectures by intelligent teachers, one can make a dangerous mistake. Unfortunately, we haven't avoided this mistake. Economic miscalculations, discrepancies between words and deeds, and wishful thinking have brought moral losses and created a moral vacuum. Drug addiction has sprouted from this ground.[49]

Although many of these explanations may have merit, the nascent state of the etiology of drug abuse in the USSR is obvious. Officials may be recognising that this circumstance precludes an effective response to drug abuse. Former Deputy Prime Minister Alexandra Biryukova, speaking at an international conference on drug trafficking, admitted that 'decisive successes' had eluded the Soviet antidrug programme 'because we fought against the results, not against the causes and symptoms' of the problem. Reducing demand for drugs requires an accurate appraisal of why they are abused, Biryukova contended.

> We proceed from the fact that drug addiction is born from the social and cultural conditions of life, and only then from the coca and poppy plantations and the chemical laboratories . . . it is necessary to turn to face man directly and investigate in depth what it is precisely in his communal and individual makeup, in his spiritual environment, which causes a craving for drugs.[50]

Table 3.2   Sources of narcotics for known drug users in the
Georgian SSR
(1984–5)

Source*	Drug users supplied by source** (per cent)
Black market	70.2
Comrades	53.1
Friends and acquaintances	39.6
Persons working in:	
Pharmacies	16.7
Medical institutions	15.1
Veterinary institutions	1.2
Relatives	4.5
Personal manufacture	14.4

 * The commentary on the study did not make clear the distinction between
several sources, for example, 'comrades' and 'friends and acquaintances' –
that seemingly may overlap one another.
** Some respondents gave several responses.

Source: *Sotsiologicheskie issledovaniya*, no. 1, 1987, p. 52.

ACQUIRING DRUGS

Individuals so inclined can acquire drugs in multiple ways (see Table
3.2). Most commonly, they purchase drugs from professional traffickers in this trade. A senior official in the USSR MVD, reversing
long-standing official silence on the subject, recently charged that a
'Narco-Mafia' of organised drug dealers and pushers dominated the
illicit trade in drugs in the Soviet Union.[51] The 'most conservative'
estimate placed the profits of this trade to the narco-mafia at two
billion roubles annually, while other estimates more than double this
figure.[52] Not surprisingly, law enforcement officials responsible for
combating this illegality may themselves become 'caught in the cling-
ing web that is the drug trade and allow traffickers to operate with
impunity'.[53]

The vast areas where poppies and hemp grow wild or are cultivated
either legally by collective farmers or illegally by 'hundreds of
thousands' of households are a major source of raw materials for
drugs.[54] The poppy harvest supposedly is reserved exclusively for the
production of legal drugs and for culinary purposes. However, it is
freely admitted that much of the crop is sold on the black market to

organised drug manufacturers and individuals who produce opium-based derivatives from it. Collective farmers often more than double their incomes through the lucrative trade in poppies.[55] By one estimate, upwards of 50 per cent of the hemp and poppy crop grown legally on collective farms remains in the fields after harvesting and becomes a fertile source of drugs for both local users and illegal drug producers.[56]

Pharmacies, hospitals, and other medical establishments provide another source of drugs for illicit use. Reportedly, such institutions are the principal source for illicit drugs of 30–40 per cent of the drug abusers in Leningrad, Moscow, and the Baltic Republics.[57] They acquire the drugs either by stealing them or using fraudulent prescriptions, or by purchasing stolen drugs from personnel employed in these institutions. Ironically, such practices seemingly have increased as drug abusers respond to stricter controls over the cultivation of poppies and hemp by seeking alternative sources for drugs.[58]

Smugglers, either amateur or professional, also supply drugs for domestic consumption. The thousands of foreign tourists and students who annually visit the former USSR and may bring with them drugs to sell or give to local friends and acquaintances mostly comprise the former category.[59] Professional traffickers either smuggle drugs directly into the Soviet Union or ship drugs from Asia and the Middle East *via* the Soviet Union to Western Europe and the United States. Reportedly, a thriving trade has developed between smugglers from Afghanistan and Iran and Soviet drug abusers, in which the latter acquire drugs for coveted commodities, including video equipment, furs, icons, weapons, and even automobiles.[60]

Soviet sources themselves usually contend that strict controls at borders over the movement of both goods and individuals substantially limit this smuggling. Several recent accounts dispute this. One source – while providing no data on volume – admitted that smuggled drugs do enter the USSR through 'chinks' in its customs service.[61] Another source, perhaps hyperbolically, charged that insufficient manpower and equipment in the customs service had made Soviet borders 'virtually open' to drug traffickers. 'Casual unscrupulous people' among the ranks of customs officials also abetted the illicit trade in drugs.[62] The overall volume of drugs smuggled into the USSR remains unknown, although one source claims that these drugs may account for upwards of 20 per cent of the drugs that Soviet abusers consume annually.[63]

Finally, abusers satisfy their habit through the use of commodities

Table 3.3   Monthly expenditures on illegal drugs by known drug users in
the Georgian SSR
(1984–5)

Expenditure (in roubles)	Per cent of those surveyed
Up to 20	2.3
20–50	5.9
50–100	10.8
100–200	11.8
200–300	6.5
300–500	8.4
500–1000	13.7
1000–3000	22.2
No answer	18.4
	100.0

Source: *Sotsiologicheskie issledovaniya*, no. 1, 1987, p. 51.

obtained legally. They inhale volatile substances (for example, glue
and paint remover), they swallow brews of legitimate medicines
mixed with alcohol or strong teas, and they produce synthetic or
semi-synthetic drugs from available chemicals and other in-
gredients.[64]

Definitive generalisations cannot be made about expenditures on
illicit drugs in the former USSR. However, the data available do
suggest that for many individuals these expenditures each month
substantially exceed the average monthly wage of a Soviet worker
(see Table 3.3). Drug users resort to assorted illegalities to acquire
these sums. In 1989, administrative proceedings were instituted
against more than 65 000 citizens for sundry offenses 'related to drug
addiction'.[65] Most violations involve the illicit production or distribution of drugs while the remainder comprise assorted illegalities –
theft, prostitution, the use of forged prescriptions – to acquire money
for, or directly obtain, drugs. To these ends, drug addicts are reportedly responsible in 'some regions' for upwards of 60 per cent of
all burglaries of apartments.[66] Even murder is not unknown in the
drug trade: 'We are seeing drug possession, payment for drugs, and
large debts as motives for murder. Incidents of this kind are primarily
taking place in Central Asia'.[67]

THE RESPONSE

The Soviet Union, by acknowledging its existence, has now taken the requisite first step to combat drug abuse. Since 1986, the USSR Supreme Soviet, the USSR Supreme Court, and the Procurator General of both the USSR and the Russian Republic have held official sessions on this subject.[68] In 1988, the USSR Ministry of Public Health began publishing *Voprosy narkologii*, a quarterly journal devoted to research on drug and alcohol abuse.[69] The Komsomol subsequently established a commission to combat social pathologies – including drug abuse – among young people.[70] Of course, not everyone acknowledges the seriousness of drug abuse. Many personnel in the MVD charged with combating drug abuse reportedly still believe that 'in some parts of the country there is absolutely no drug abuse whatsoever'. This 'delusion', as one source characterises it, helps explain why these personnel move 'slowly' and do a 'poor job' in their work.[71]

Numerous Soviet sources admit that the battle against drug abuse has just begun.[72] Anti-drug initiatives still are often subsumed under institutions and policies concerned primarily with alcoholism and mental health rather than specifically with drug abuse. Considerable debate also exists among specialists regarding the most effective means to combat drug abuse. Punitive measures predominate among initiatives that have been undertaken. The director of a drug clinic explains why:

> The drug addict is a socially dangerous person. . . . What we need is strict police control, registration, official hospital treatment and complete frankness about the issue. If you want to be a full fledged member of society, prove it by your actions.[73]

Legal strictures against drugs reflect these sentiments. Under the Criminal Code of the Russian Republic, the illegal manufacture, acquisition, storage and transport of narcotic substances with intent to sell or actual sale are punishable by deprivation of freedom for up to ten years (with or without confiscation of property). These acts, when committed without intent to sell, entail deprivation of freedom for up to three years or, in the case of recidivists, for up to five years. The Criminal Code also specifies criminal liability for the planting or cultivation of forbidden crops that are considered to contain narcotic substances (for example, poppies and several types of hemp), establishing places for the use of narcotics, and the habitual consumption of narcotics.[74]

These penalties in the republic of Georgia are even harsher.[75] Activities associated with intent to sell, or the actual sale of, narcotic substances entail deprivation of freedom for up to 15 years with confiscation of property. Persons using or attempting to use narcotic substances without a doctor's prescription can be imprisoned for 10 to 15 days. The criminal codes of Kirgizia and Uzbekistan contain similar provisions against the use of narcotics, while all other union republics punish the act administratively by fine. Turkmenistan until November 1987 maintained criminal penalties – prison terms for up to one year or corrective labour for up to two years – for the use of narcotics.[76]

Between 1985 and 1987, an average of 28.6 thousand individuals were convicted annually for sundry 'narcotic-related' crimes.[77] In 1988 and 1989, 14.4 thousand and 12.2 thousand individuals, respectively, were convicted of such offences.[78] Soviet sources offer no convincing explanation for the substantial decline in convictions in the latter years. Indictments for drug related offences usually entail 'little things' involving the possession and/or use of illicit narcotic substances.[79] Courts usually sentence individuals convicted of the illegal manufacture, acquisition, storage, and transport of narcotic substances with intent to sell to deprivation of freedom for one or two years.[80]

Critics express considerable dissatisfaction with these measures. One criticism alleges that legal strictures minimally deter drug abuse either because judges are overly lenient in applying existing sanctions or, paradoxically, because the sanctions themselves are insufficiently stringent.[81]

Ironically, other critics charge that judges are overly harsh in their actions. Such critics oppose the common practice of applying criminal sanctions entailing deprivation of freedom to individuals convicted of possession for personal use of small quantities of drugs, including hashish and marijuana.[82] According to Professor Gabiani, incarceration can turn casual drug users into hardened addicts by placing them in prison conditions where illicit drugs are readily available and many fellow inmates are addicts.[83] Others argue that it is inhumane and no deterrent to incarcerate individuals for acts their addiction compels them to commit.[84] Official policy appears to be moving towards decriminalisation of casual drug use. Reportedly, the USSR MVD no longer institutes criminal proceedings against people for possession of small quantities of illicit drugs, or if they voluntarily submit themselves to the authorities.[85] Further, guidelines issued recently by the USSR Supreme Court imply a less harsh approach to the casual use of drugs, especially non-narcotic ones.[86]

The USSR MVD received considerable criticism for its alleged laxity in enforcing legislation against drugs.[87] Critics allege that the agency exhibits 'serious shortcomings' in this work, its criminal investigation units are 'weak' and their initiative 'low', and local cadres do little to expose participants in the illegal drug trade. While the police annually uncover 'tens of thousands' of drug-related crimes, drug traffickers comprise only a small percentage of individuals apprehended therein. A senior USSR MVD official estimates that police confiscate 'only' 15–20 per cent of the illicit drugs in the USSR.[88]

Several factors account for these failings. As noted, many officials charged with the enforcement of anti-drug legislation have themselves become participants in the illegal drug trade. Even honest policemen often are ineffective in combating drug-related illegalities, because they receive almost no specialised training and possess inadequate equipment for this task.[89] The political fragmentation now affecting the former USSR represents a new variable that could undermine the fight against drugs by preventing what officials consider the requisite centralisation for this effort.[90]

Several well-publicised campaigns to reduce the size of, or limit access to, the poppy and hemp crop have proven particularly ineffective:

> We attack it wherever we can; we cut it, burn it, treat it with herbicides, and plough it under. We made all the farmers promise to work to exterminate it. And we created special units to fight it. . . . But all of these measures are not very effective.[91]

Efforts by Soviet specialists to develop new varieties of hemp with minimal narcotic content have proven equally unsuccessful.[92] Available evidence suggests that the recent decision to discontinue legal cultivation of certain types of poppies (and rely upon importation to meet demand for culinary and medicinal purposes) will not appreciably limit the availability of illegal drugs.[93] Some specialists now argue that abuse of drugs (although not their sale or distribution) is a medical, not a legal, problem and should be treated accordingly. Reflecting this attitude, a senior official in the USSR MVD commented that 'society does not gain when, instead of trying to treat a patient, we send him to a corrective labour camp'.[94]

To encourage drug users to seek therapy, officials have pledged that those doing so voluntarily will incur no criminal liability (although they will be registered with the police and must undergo therapy).[95] In contrast, a proposal to prohibit drug 'addicts' to marry until they have successfully completed requisite therapy seems unlikely to encourage voluntary resort to treatment.[96] A similar observation applies to the requirement that those undergoing voluntary treatment must register with the police. As one drug treatment specialist contends (plausibly), 'you'll agree that hardly anyone is likely to seek advice when they know they will be immediately registered with the police'.[97] The USSR Supreme Court recently instructed courts to 'consider' compulsory treatment for drug addicts who refuse voluntary treatment. Addicts undergo such treatment in 'closed-type therapy and labour rehabilitation centres' run by the police. Inmates receive wages for labour performed (which are used to help defray the costs they incur for their treatment), but those who attempt escape are subject to prison terms of up to one year.[98]

Reportedly, in 1987 over 80 per cent of the registered addicts underwent either voluntary or compulsory drug addiction therapy. Officials claim that almost 40 per cent of the individuals who underwent voluntary treatment have now 'stopped using narcotics'.[99] These claims merit caution. First, the Russian Republic Minister of Public Health reports that in 1986 only 25 per cent of the registered drug addicts in the USSR received any medical treatment whatsoever for their condition.[100] Indeed, in 1988 only 31 hospitals and 410 clinics in the USSR provided treatment for abuse of drugs.[101] Second, few, if any, treatment programmes for drug abuse anywhere can boast the alleged rate of success of Soviet programmes. Third, it may be premature to claim permanent success for treatment when, as Soviet sources frankly admit, many so-called 'cured' addicts soon revert to drugs.[102] Finally, considerable evidence exists that drug treatment facilities and procedures are woefully inadequate to their task.

The Russian Republic Minister of Public Health has been outspoken on this latter subject.[103] He claims there are 'no physicians in the USSR who know how to treat drug addicts properly' (in part, because few medical schools offer training in this area). The addicts who are treated usually receive an ineffectual 'high speed' treatment of 7 to 8 days. The Minister himself recommends that treatment extend for 'at least' 60 days with continued close supervision of the addict upon completion of formal therapy. He also feels 'in no uncertain terms' that the alcohol abuse clinics where drug addicts typically receive treatment have proven unsuited for this purpose. His overall assessment of drug treatment is blunt: 'As yet, there is no effective therapy for drug addiction' in the former USSR. To help remedy this condition, officials have urged the utilisation of drug treatment practices successfully employed abroad.[104]

Efforts to alert the population to the dangers of drugs constitute another body of measures. Typically, these measures have been overly heavy-handed and didactic. Television documentaries about drug abuse have such titles as 'Children of Vice', 'Pain', and 'Business Trip to Hell'. An article entitled 'A Warning', describing the horrors of drug addiction, appeared in a mass circulation weekly. At one point, a young addict calls the individual who supplies him with drugs 'My Mephistopheles' and adds that 'as a rule, drug addicts are a cowardly but inquisitive lot'.[105] Three million copies of an informational pamphlet about drugs, 'Beware of the White Cloud', will be used in Soviet schools.[106] Survey research conducted in secondary schools in Moscow found that anti-drug propaganda had little credibility with students, who saw it as hyperbolic and incongruent with their own experiences with drugs.[107] Then, too, 'many people' refuse even to discuss the problem of drug abuse. In one instance, a conference of educators prevented doctors from addressing them about drug abuse 'on the pretext that there were more important problems and the topic was not appropriate for a wide audience'.[108]

Finally, the USSR has begun to co-operate with other states to combat drug abuse. This co-operation – although still limited – reverses the traditional official attitude that saw drug abuse as a problem principally for capitalist states. While the Soviet Union is a signatory to both the 1961 United Nations' Uniform Convention on Narcotics and the 1971 United Nations' Convention on Psychotropic Substances, it has fulfilled their obligations only perfunctorily.[109]

Since 1988, the USSR has concluded agreements to combat international drug trafficking with many western states, including Canada, the Federal Republic of Germany, France, Great Britain, Italy, Spain and the United States.[110] Reportedly, the Soviet Union has shared intelligence with the United States and other western nations that has resulted in the seizure of illegal drugs and the arrest of traffickers. The USSR has proposed that such co-operation be formalised in an agreement between itself and the United States Drug Enforcement Agency.[111] This latter agency has now begun to train Soviet personnel in drug enforcement skills.[112] The Soviet Union has become a member of Interpol, the international police organisation intimately involved in the fight against drugs,[113] and was an active participant in the 1987 United Nations' sponsored conference on drug abuse held in Vienna.[114] It has supported a proposal before the United Nations General Assembly to establish an international criminal court with jurisdiction over cases of drug trafficking between countries.[115] Finally, the USSR and the then communist regimes of Eastern Europe held two conferences (in 1987 and 1988) to co-ordinate efforts to interdict international drug trafficking.[116] The conclusion of an agreement to the same end with the non-communist government of Czechoslovakia in February 1990 suggests that the individual republics are prepared to continue such co-operation even after the demise of communism in Eastern Europe.[117]

Of course, the most controversial aspect of this subject is the allegation of the United States that the Soviet Union and its allies engaged in drug trafficking to earn hard currency and undermine the moral fabric of western societies. One recent study, co-authored by a defector who had been a senior officer in the Czechoslovak armed forces, asserts that the Soviets began thinking about this when they discovered widespread use of drugs among US troops during the Korean War. Reportedly, this discovery led Soviet analysts to conclude that drugs could be employed as a long-term strategic weapon to cripple capitalist societies. Nikita Khrushchev allegedly justified the morality of this strategy by asserting that 'anything that speeds the destruction of capitalism is moral'.[118]

Recently published information lends credence to these allegations. An article published in the newspaper of the democratic opposition in Bulgaria – and summarised in an English language dispatch by the official Bulgarian newsagency – asserts that Bulgaria was a 'central operator' under the communist regime of Todor Zhivkov in trading narcotics for weapons. A desire for profit and a determination to destabilise western societies primarily motivated this trade, the article charges.[119] An even more sensational charge accuses former leaders of the East German Communist Party, including Erich Honecker, its former Secretary General, of personal involvement in this same trade and for the same ends.[120] Allegedly, this lucrative trade (conducted with the knowledge and active complicity of the USSR) continued throughout Honecker's nearly twenty-year tenure as Secretary General and brought him profits of approximately $75 million.

PROSPECTS

Considerable uncertainty surrounds the present and future status of drug abuse in the USSR. Is the phenomenon as rapidly growing as many commentaries suggest, or does greater official *glasnost'* on the subject only make it appear so? One can only respond confidently that abuse of narcotics and other non-alcoholic psychotropic substances lags far behind alcohol as the most abused drug in the USSR.

A definitive etiology of drug abuse still awaits development in the USSR. More sophisticated analyses of this subject are now appearing in such specialised journals as *Voprosy narkologii*. Will the seemingly more conservative political trend evident in the early 1990s persist and inhibit scholarly inquiry into this (and other socially sensitive) topics? The answer will prove a key variable determining the effectiveness of future efforts to combat drug abuse in the former USSR.

These efforts themselves are the subject of intense debate. The different approaches to the problem are readily discernible in the specialised and popular literature on the subject. Most fundamentally, debate involves those who see drug abuse as primarily a criminal act to be combated with punitive measures and those who perceive it as an illness to be treated therapeutically. Policies reflecting each approach – for example, the 'hard line' policy of compulsory treatment of drug 'addicts' and the 'soft line' policy of decriminalisation of casual use of non-narcotic drugs – now characterise Soviet efforts to combat drug abuse.

This analysis may evoke *déjà vu* among Western readers as they survey the drug problem in their own countries. Surely they will encounter uncertainty about the incidence of drug abuse, contending theories about why individuals resort to drugs, and often bitter polemics regarding the most efficacious means to combat the problem. Hopefully the states that constitute the new Commonwealth can learn from the experiences, and avoid the mistakes, of their Western counterparts in the fight against drugs. Failure to do so could find them in a sisyphean endeavour to combat 'narcomania'.

Notes

1. Among the few previous analyses of this subject in English are E. A. Babaian, 'Control of Narcotic Substances and Prevention of Addiction

in the USSR', *Bulletin on Narcotics*, January–March 1979, pp. 13–22; David E. Powell, 'Drug Abuse in Communist Europe', *Problems of Communism*, July–August 1973, pp. 31–40; John M. Kramer, 'Drug Abuse in the Soviet Union', *Problems of Communism*, March–April 1988, pp. 28–40.

2. *New Times*, no. 22, May 1984, p. 27; Radio Moscow, 4 April 1985 in Foreign Broadcast Information Service–*Soviet Union Daily Report* ('FBIS-SOV'), 8 April 1985, R3.

3. All materials in this paragraph drawn from *Sotsiologicheskie issledovaniya*, no. 4, 1989, p. 57.

4. *Sovetskoe gosudarstvo i pravo*, no. 1, 1987, in *Soviet Law and Government*, Summer 1988, p. 26. All materials on anti-drug legislation in the 1920s and 1930s are drawn from this source.

5. *Izvestiya*, 3 March 1966 and 26 November 1966.

6. *Literaturnaya gazeta*, 26 October 1988.

7. *Vedomosti Verkhovnogo Soveta SSSR*, 31 May 1972, item 176; *Vedomosti Verkhovnogo Soveta RSFSR*, 31 August 1972, item 870.

8. *Vedomosti Verkhovnogo Soveta SSSR*, 1 May 1974, item 275.

9. *Literaturnaya gazeta*, 15 October 1975. The report on the session itself is carried in *Izvestiya*, 9 October 1975.

10. *Izvestiya*, 12 August 1986.

11. See *Moscow News*, no. 24, 1990, p. 15 for a discussion of this research.

12. Ibid.

13. *Sovetskoe gosudarstvo i pravo*, no. 7, 1987, p. 66. In contrast, an earlier broadcast on Radio Moscow asserted that in the USSR the consumption of opiates such as heroin and morphine was 'practically unheard of except for foreign films'. Radio Moscow, 30 August 1986 in FBIS–*SOV*, 3 September 1986, R4.

14. *Bakinskii rabochii*, 26 August 1986.

15. See, for example, the interview with the Minister of Public Health of the Russian Republic in *Literaturnaya gazeta*, 20 August 1986.

16. Quoted in *The Washington Post*, 11 August 1986.

17. For an extended discussion of this circumstance, see Second Report of the National Commission on Marijuana and Drug Abuse, *Drug Use in America: Problem in Perspective* (Washington, DC: Government Printing Office, 1973) pp. 121–140. Another treatment of this subject is R. L. Hartnoll, 'Current Situation Related to Drug Abuse Assessment in European Countries', *Bulletin on Narcotics*, January–June 1986, especially pp. 71–6.

18. *Sovetskoe gosudarstvo i pravo*, no. 5, 1988, p. 93.

19. 'Narcotics' medically are defined as central nervous system depressants with analgesic and sedative properties. Under United States federal law, narcotics are considered to be addictive drugs that produce physical and psychological dependence and include opium and its derivatives, heroin, morphine, codeine, and several synthetic substances which can produce morphine-type addiction. Under this conception of narcotics, hashish and marijuana would be excluded. Robert O'Brien and Sidney Cohen (eds), *The Encyclopedia of Drug Abuse* (New York: Facts on File, 1984), p. 183.

20. Babaian, 'Control of Narcotic Substances', p. 18.
21. *Izvestiya*, 28 June 1989.
22. *Sovetskoe gosudarstvo i pravo*, no. 1, 1987, in *Soviet Law and Government*, Summer 1988, p. 36.
23. *Izvestiya*, 30 August 1990.
24. *Moscow News*, no. 24, 1990, p. 15.
25. Powell, 'Drug Abuse in Communist Europe', found that drug abuse was restricted primarily to the progeny of the middle and higher classes resident in urban areas.
26. In the aforementioned study of drug use by Professor Gabiani, only 3.6 per cent of the users surveyed consumed cocaine, while the respective figure for heroin was 1.2 per cent. In contrast, upwards of 29 per cent of the users named opium as their drug of choice. Over half of the users in the survey (53.3 per cent) primarily consumed hashish. *Moscow News*, no. 24, 1990, p. 15.
27. Ibid.
28. *Izvestiya*, 30 August 1990.
29. *Moscow News*, no. 24, 1990, p. 15.
30. *Izvestiya*, 30 August 1990.
31. *Izvestiya*, 13 May 1987.
32. The pharmacology of hashish is discussed in O'Brien and Cohen, *The Encyclopedia of Drug Abuse*, pp. 117–119.
33. *Izvestiya*, 10 March 1988.
34. *Izvestiya*, 30 August 1990.
35. For an accusation that the fight against drugs has assumed the character of a 'campaign' similar to those against alcoholism and unearned incomes, see *Moscow News*, no. 34, 1988, p. 13.
36. All materials on this research are drawn from *Sovetskoe gosudarstvo i pravo*, no. 7, 1987, p. 64–9. See also *Zarya vostoka*, 20 February 1987; *Sotsiologicheskie issledovaniya*, no. 1, 1987, pp. 48–53.
37. A compilation of these theories appears in O'Brien and Cohen, *The Encyclopedia of Drug Abuse*, especially pp. 274–9.
38. For a typical exposition of this argument, see *Sovetskoe gosudarstvo i pravo*, no. 5, 1988, p. 86.
39. *Literaturnaya gazeta*, 20 August 1986.
40. *Sovetskoe gosudarstvo i pravo*, no. 1, 1990, p. 72.
41. For a typical exposition of this argument, see *Bakinskii rabochii*, 26 August 1986.
42. *Sovetskoe gosudarstvo i pravo*, no. 1, 1990, p. 69.
43. *Komsomol'skaya pravda*, 25 April 1990.
44. For example, polling data from the Georgian SSR indicate that 90 per cent of the drug users surveyed 'did not know about the pernicious consequences of narcotics when they reached for the poison the first time'. *Izvestiya*, 12 August 1986. A similar argument is made in *Uchitel'skaya gazeta*, 10 January 1987. The statement by the drug treatment specialist that any illicit drug use can lead to tragedy is reported by *Moscow Domestic Service*, 15 December 1987 in FBIS–SOV, 18 December 1987, p. 42.
45. See, for example, *Komsomol'skaya pravda*, 8 June 1986, and *Moskov-*

skaya pravda, 12 June 1986. On the other hand, the deputy head of the Main Administration for Criminal Investigation of the USSR MVD asserts that no definitive data establish a link between increased consumption of illicit drugs and Gorbachev's anti-alcoholism campaign. *Literaturnaya gazeta*, 20 August 1986. Lending credence to this assessment, numerous reports indicate that the Gorbachev campaign has encountered serious obstacles and done little to reduce the overall consumption of alcohol in the USSR. Indeed, it is far more likely that the campaign has stimulated the consumption of *samogon* – that is, 'moonshine' – rather than illicit drugs. On the problems encountered in the anti-alcoholism campaign see, for example, *Izvestiya*, 3 October 1987.

46. *Sobesednik*, no. 2, January 1988. Interviews with Soviet soldiers who had served in Afghanistan make clear 'that obtaining hashish, opium or other narcotics from the local Afghan population was no problem at all' for these soldiers. *Literaturnaya gazeta*, 26 October 1988. For an overall discussion of drug abuse in the Soviet military, see *Krasnaya zvezda*, 28 November 1987.
47. *Moscow News*, no. 50, 1988, p. 15. This source asserts that similar practices also occur in school athletics: 'Drugs are also well known to some victors in school competitions'.
48. *Ogonek*, no. 23, 1989.
49. *Sobesednik*, no. 40, September 1986.
50. *Moscow Domestic Service*, 15 April 1990 in FBIS–*SOV*, 16 April 1990, p. 59.
51. This official elaborates: 'No matter what we call it, the Narco-Mafia or an organized criminal group . . . coherent professional group crime does exist and has for a long time'. *Moscow Television Service*, 19 February 1988 in FBIS–*SOV*, 26 February 1988, p. 62.
52. *Moscow News*, no. 24, 1990, p. 15.
53. *Pravda*, 18 February 1988; *Izvestiya*, 12 February 1990. This circumstance is not surprising given the recent report by the Minister of the USSR MVD revealing widespread corruption among ministerial personnel. The Minister reports that between 1983 and 1985 approximately 160 000 employees in the agency were dismissed 'for violation of law and order, for their being unable to attend to their duties'. *TASS*, 26 March 1988 in FBIS–*SOV*, 5 April 1988, p. 48.
54. *Izvestiya*, 6 October 1987 carries the comment that 'hundreds of thousands' of households illegally grow poppies and hemp.
55. *Komsomol'skaia pravda*, 8 June 1986.
56. *Literaturnaya gazeta*, 20 August 1986.
57. As reported by the head of the Main Administration for Criminal Investigation of the USSR MVD in *Izvestiya*, 29 February 1988.
58. *Pravda*, 17 February 1988.
59. For an accusation that such practices occur, see *Moscow Domestic Service*, 29 January 1988 in FBIS–*SOV*, 2 February 1988, p. 63.
60. *Izvestiya*, 12 February 1990.
61. The comment regarding 'chinks' in the customs service comes from *Pravda*, 3 February 1988. This especially appears to be a problem in the

Turkmenian SSR which borders on both Afghanistan and Iran: 'The situation is worsened there by the closeness of the state border. It becomes necessary to check on the border areas and close all loopholes to prevent the taking of narcotics into the republic from outside'. (*TASS*, 15 April 1988 in FBIS–*SOV*, 19 April 1988.)

62. *Izvestiya*, 30 May 1988 charges that Soviet borders are 'virtually open' to traffickers and that 'casual unscrupulous people' fill the ranks of the customs service.
63. *Izvestiya*, 25 July 1990.
64. On these practices, see *Izvestiya*, 26 March 1988.
65. *Krasnaya zvezda*, 14 February 1990.
66. *Izvestiya*, 29 February 1988.
67. Ibid.
68. For reports of these sessions, see, respectively, *Izvestiya*, 5 March 1988, *Izvestiya*, 1 January 1988 and *Sovetskaya Rossiya*, 26 December 1986.
69. Rubrics under which articles are published include 'Biological Aspects of Narcology', 'Diagnosis', 'Clinical Narcology', 'Epidemiology', 'Guidelines for Practitioners', and 'Practical Notes'. Articles published in the first several issues have examined both physiological and sociological aspects of drug and alcohol abuse.
70. *Moscow Domestic Service*, 29 January 1988 in FBIS–*SOV*, 2 February 1988, p. 63.
71. These remarks came from the head of the Main Administration for Criminal Investigation of the USSR MVD. *Izvestiya*, 29 February 1988.
72. For example, one source recently asserted that drug abuse has demonstrated an 'uncommon ability' to resist efforts to eradicate it. *Pravda*, 17 February 1988. In the opinion of another source, 'we have virtually no means of combating this evil'. *Komsomol'skaya pravda*, 3 March 1988.
73. *Ogonek*, no. 8, February 1988.
74. For a detailed discussion of anti-drug legislation in the USSR, see *Meditsinskaya gazeta*, 9 April 1986. The relevant articles in the Criminal Code of the Russian Republic are nos. 224–6.
75. *Sovetskoe gosudarstvo i pravo*, no. 7, 1987, pp. 67–9 provides an extended analysis of this legislation. The relevant article in the Criminal Code of the Georgian SSR is no. 252.
76. *TASS*, 19 November 1987, cited in Radio Liberty, *Research Bulletin*, no. 473, 20 November 1987.
77. The USSR State Committee for Statistics reports that in 1985, 1986, and 1987 there were, respectively, 25.6, 33.6, and 26.8 thousand individuals convicted for such offences. *Argumenty i fakty*, 12 November 1988, p. 6.
78. *Sotsial'noe razvitie SSSR* (Moscow: Finansy i Statistika, 1990) p. 329.
79. *Izvestiya*, 29 February 1988.
80. This figure comes from a survey of court practice reported in *Sovetskoe gosudarstvo i pravo*, no. 7, 1987, p. 69.
81. For example, Professor Gabiani reports that courts in Soviet Georgia 'frequently' apply to drug dealers (even including 'organized criminal dealers of narcotics') the less stringent sanctions intended for those who

only use, but do not sell, narcotics. The courts take the path of least resistance', in Gabiani's opinion, because they do not want 'to trouble themselves with the complex procedures for demonstration of guilt in the sale of narcotics'. Ibid., pp. 67–8.

82. See, for example, the commentary in *Moscow News*, 19 August 1987.
83. *Sovetskoe gosudarstvo i pravo*, no. 7, 1987, p. 67.
84. *Sovetskoe gosudarstvo i pravo*, no. 1, 1987, in *Soviet Law and Government*, Summer 1988, p. 34.
85. *Izvestiya*, 29 February 1988.
86. The guidelines instruct courts to consider in such cases not only the quantity of drugs involved but also the 'characteristics of the varying kinds of narcotics in terms of the degree of their effect on the human body'. *Izvestiya*, 1 January 1988. Another source reports that recent amendments and supplements to the criminal law on drug addiction establish standards for 'smaller quantities of drugs'–although it does not indicate what drugs come under the new standards. *Moscow Television Service*, 11 January 1988 in FBIS–*SOV*, 19 January 1988, p. 64.
87. Unless otherwise noted, all materials in this paragraph are drawn from interviews with the Minister of the USSR MVD and the head of the Main Administration for Criminal Investigation of the USSR MVD published in, respectively, *Pravda*, 6 January 1987 and *Izvestiya*, 29 February 1988.
88. *Izvestiya*, 30 August 1990.
89. *Komsomol'skaya pravda*, 8 June 1986.
90. *Izvestiya*, 30 August 1990. This is the opinion of the Chief of the Main Criminal Investigation Administration, USSR MVD. Of course, some might interpret this as the self-serving argument of an official far more interested in preserving the political integrity of the Soviet state than in combating drug abuse.
91. *Izvestiya*, 30 June 1986.
92. This effort is proceeding 'slowly', according to the Minister of the USSR MVD. *Pravda*, 6 January 1987.
93. *TASS*, 16 February 1988 in FBIS–*SOV*, 24 February 1988, p. 54, carries an announcement of this decision. REportedly, this decision was 'not reached easily' as several agencies argued that the poppy had too many economic uses to ban its cultivation. *Izvestiya*, 6 October 1987. Available evidence indicates that drug users have responded to the ban on poppy cultivation by consuming other types of drugs. One source contends: 'The results were not as expected. Many addicts have started using chemical compounds, medicines, and tranquilizers. There has been a sharp rise in substance abuse'. *Trud*, 3 August 1988.
94. *Literaturnaya gazeta*, 20 August 1986. For expressions of similar sentiments, see, for example, *Izvestiya*, 12 August 1986; *Komsomol'skaya pravda*, 11 January 1987.
95. *Moskovskaya pravda*, 12 June 1986.
96. This proposal was made in a round-table discussion of initiatives to combat drug abuse as published in *Sovetskoe gosudarstvo i pravo*, no. 8, 1987, p. 138.
97. *Ogonek*, no. 8, February 1988.

98. For a detailed discussion of this treatment, see *Krasnaya zvezda*, 28 April 1990.
99. *TASS*, 16 February 1988 in FBIS–*SOV*, 24 February 1988, p. 54; *Izvestiya*, 29 February 1988; *Moscow Television Service*, 19 February 1988 in FBIS–*SOV*, 26 February 1988, p. 62.
100. *Literaturnaya gazeta*, 20 August 1986.
101. *Trud*, 3 August 1988.
102. See, for example, *Sovetskoe gosudarstvo i pravo*, no. 8, 1987, p. 137; *Literaturnaya gazeta*, 20 August 1986. One study found that 'at best' only 10 per cent of the treated addicts were permanently cured of their habit. *Ogonek*, no. 8, February 1988.
103. The following discussion is drawn from the interview with the Minister published in *Literaturnaya gazeta*, 20 August 1986.
104. *TASS*, 16 February 1988 in FBIS–*SOV*, 24 February 1988, p. 55.
105. On the television documentaries about drug abuse, see *Izvestiya*, 12 August 1986. The article 'A Warning' appeared in *Nedelya*, 12 January 1986 in FBIS–*SOV*, 17 January 1986, R2–3.
106. The contents of the pamphlet are discussed in *Uchite'skaya gazeta*, 15 January 1987. For a highly critical assessment of the work of educational institutions in alerting their students to the dangers of drugs, see *Sovetskaya Rossiya*, 26 December 1986.
107. The results of the survey conducted among a 'representative' sample of 134 students enrolled in secondary schools in Moscow are reported in *Sotsiologicheskie issledovaniya*, no. 3, 1989, pp. 69–70. For a detailed indictment of anti-drug propaganda among youths, see *Voprosy narkologii*, no. 1, 1990, p. 54.
108. *Sovetskaya Rossiya*, 31 August 1986. At times, parents have resisted efforts by teachers to inform them of the drug-related activities of their progeny. For examples of such behaviour, see *Sobesednik*, no. 4, September 1986.
109. For an analysis of these conventions by a Soviet author, see L. N. Anisimov, *Narkotiki: Pravovoi rezhim* (Leningrad: Izdatel'stvo Leningradskogo Universiteta, 1974), pp. 34–54, 63–72.
110. For a discussion of these agreements, see *Sovetskaya molodezh'*, 5 June 1990. The USSR has also concluded such agreements with Argentina, Austria, and Cyprus.
111. *The Washington Post*, 20 July 1988, provides details of the proposal. The Director of the Drug Enforcement Agency asserts that such co-operation would bring 'minimal' benefits to the United States, but the proposal should be considered because 'the drug problem is an international problem and the more countries that co-operate the better for all of us'. Ibid., 21 February 1988, provides information on multilateral efforts involving the Soviet Union and Western states undertaken to date to interdict international drug trafficking. See *The New York Times*, 1 May 1988 for an example of where Soviet assistance facilitated the seizure by British authorities of 3.5 tons of hashish.
112. *The Washington Post*, 21 February 1988.
113. *Moscow Domestic Service*, 28 September 1990 in FBIS–*SOV*, 28 September 1990, p. 14.

114. *Sotsialisticheskaya industriya*, 16 September 1987 discusses the participation of the USSR in the conference.
115. *TASS*, 12 September 1989 in FBIS–*SOV*, 12 September 1989, p. 35.
116. The first conference, involving representatives from all states of Communist Europe (except Yugoslavia), plus Cuba and Mongolia, met in Sofia, Bulgaria in May 1987. For details of the meeting see *Bulgarska telegrafna agentsiia*, 12 May 1987 in FBIS–*East Europe Daily Report*, 14 May 1987, AA2. The second meeting took place in June 1988 in the USSR. The participants, the respective Ministers of Internal Affairs from Bulgaria, Czechoslovakia, Hungary, Poland and the USSR, met to discuss 'problems connected with the anti-drug struggle'. The participants signed a protocol 'on co-operation in the sphere of combating drug addiction'. They also agreed to hold 'regular meetings of this kind in the future'. See *Izvestiya*, 27 June 1988 for details of this meeting.
117. *TASS*, 26 February 1990 in FBIS–*SOV*, 27 February 1990, p. 27.
118. Joseph Douglas and Jan Sejna, 'International Narcotics Trafficking: The Soviet Connection', *Journal of Defense and Diplomacy*, December 1986, pp. 20–5. Before his defection, Sejna was secretary of the Czechoslovak Defence Council and Chief of Cabinet at the Ministry of Defence.
119. As reported by *Bulgarska telegrafna agentsiia*, 7 March 1990 in FBIS–*East Europe Daily Report*, 21 March 1990, p. 9.
120. The allegations are made by Alexander Schalck-Golodkowski, who ran East Germany's currency operations and reputedly held a high rank in the Soviet KGB. For discussion of these allegations, see *The Washington Post*, 8 March 1990. Also see *BILD* (Hamburg), 6 December 1989 in FBIS–*East Europe Daily Report*, 6 December 1989, p. 40.

4 Mortality Patterns in the USSR and Causes of Death: Political Unity and Regional Differentials

Alain Blum

Studies of Soviet mortality in the 1970s and 1980s were riven by controversy. This was especially true of trends in infant and adult mortality, of the real nature of such mortality statistics, and of the link between the medical and health systems and the general health situation in the USSR. Equally controversial were the long-term consequences of the crisis experienced by the Soviet Union as a result of the famines of the 1930s and the effects of World War II. However, recently published data now make it possible to widen the debate and to ask more specific questions about the links between a unified political structure, a common social and health system, language and structure, and the traditional social and political structures of the population, which in the main are not rooted in the system. The link between past events and the present situation has been the subject of a recent searching study by Anderson and Silver, which will be referred to in the course of the present discussion.[1]

The aim of this paper is not to study the main trends of past mortality in the USSR, but to give an overview of their present regional diversity within a geographical space larger than that of the former Soviet Union alone. The recently published data on mortality, according to causes and life-cycle tables, now allow us to compare the different republics of the Union with other countries which are culturally or geographically related.

The mortality patterns will be studied in two main respects: mortality rates according to causes in each republic of the Soviet Union as compared with other European countries, and mortality rates according to age in the 'Eastern' part of the Union (that is, Central Asia) as compared with the known structures of such rates in other developing countries. These aspects, which are only briefly examined here, permit us to ask interesting questions about the impact of more than fifty years (often of more than a century) of a single political power exercised over large, heterogeneous regions. It will be shown that despite the very real impact on the general level of mortality, patterns of mortality have maintained a remarkable continuity, and have even changed almost independently of this unity, but in the same direction as other countries situated not very far from the republics which are being studied.

It will also permit some hypotheses to be made with respect to the increase in mortality in the 1960s and 1970s in different parts of the Union. The increase might well have been the result of an insufficiently sharp decline in some causes of mortality seemingly brought about by the rigid, centrally-planned health policies, and a real evolution in the basic health structure or in the sanitary habits of the population. It is also suggested that a voluntarist and centrally-planned health policy can lead to a sharp decline in infant mortality and even of some adult mortality causes as, for example, in the case of infectious diseases. However, following a decline such a policy is insufficient to stabilise the level of mortality that has been reached, and cannot solve the problem of more developed mortality patterns. Therefore, it leads to an increase in mortality at ages where people, who have managed not to be victims of traditional causes of mortality, become the victims of new causes which the health service is incapable of combating. The well known 'period of stagnation' referred to by Soviet commentators can be seen, in the case of the health service, to have been less a period of stagnation and more an inability to change a very powerful, closed system driven by policies of centralisation and rigid planning. It is essential to have an understanding of the history of the period, as it has valuable lessons for the conducting of health policies in developing countries. However brief is this study of the problem, it does provide food for deeper reflection.

It is the author's belief, incidentally, that his hypotheses are not in conflict with the work of Anderson and Silver about cohort effects on Soviet mortality. The discussion that follows may even serve to specify those effects more precisely. But the distinction with respect to double effects appears somewhat unclear at this stage of the research, because of the lack of sufficiently precise data on infant mortality before World War II in the various parts of the Union and, indeed, because of poor data on infant mortality in general.

EUROPE AND THE USSR

In previous papers the author has, like so many others, studied the general mortality patterns of the Soviet Union.[2] The most striking conclusions have been the very high mortality of young and older adults from traumas, injuries and suicide, and the sensitivity of mortality at these ages to such short-term measures as, for example, anti-alcoholism campaigns. Mortality due to infectious diseases was also seen to be high, even if it could be explained in part by the presence of Central Asia in the statistics. However, in Russia such mortality among the younger age groups was higher in terms of its structure than in other European countries.

These studies apart, the author would now like to make a closer examination of the structure of mortality according to causes in the different republics as compared with other European countries. The mortality rates for each of the fifteen republics have been used according to age and the four main groups of causes published in *Naselenie SSSR 1988* (The Population of the USSR in 1988),[3] these being:

1. Deaths from diseases of the circulatory system (categories 25–30 of ICD–9 Basic Tabulation List).
2. Deaths from neoplasms (categories 8–17).
3. Deaths from diseases of the respiratory system (categories 310–29).
4. Deaths from accidents, adverse effects, suicide and other violent causes (categories E47–E56).

The author has computed the contribution to deaths of these four groups to the total number of deaths for each of the fifteen republics, and for the other European countries (except for the DDR, where complete data on the four groups were not published, and Denmark, where such data continue to be published according to ICD–8). The calculations were made separately for two age groups, 25–34 years and 65–74 years, on the basis of the number of deaths in each of the age groups (these are the groups used in the WHO reports), and they, indeed, appear to be very characteristic of prevailing mortality patterns.

As we have seen in a previous paper,[4] there exists a strong, almost linear relationship between the proportion of given causes of death to all causes. The author has attempted here to extract from the set of European countries, each represented by four points (for the four groups of causes distinguished above), the more representative patterns (based on a combination of two causes), and to examine the position of the Soviet republics in relation to these patterns. Only the most important conclusions are reported here. This kind of analysis would appear to be sufficient to highlight the main characteristics of the structure of mortality according to causes. The author has also attempted to undertake cluster-analysis and other multivariate analyses, but the results have not yielded more precise indications.

The strongest relationship is probably that between deaths from neoplasms and deaths from diseases of the circulatory system. In a previous article[5] this relationship was presented for standardised all-ages mortality rates and was almost linear. Again, we found that the same strong links for elderly people (65–74 years old) were almost identical for males and females. But the Soviet republics are confined within a particular zone of the plan and are characterised by a higher proportion of cardio-vascular deaths and a lower proportion of neoplasms, a phenomenon close to that of other East European countries and of some countries of Southern Europe. The patterns for the Soviet Union and more generally the East European countries appear to be very specific. This can be explained partly by the usually less-precise reporting of causes of death in these countries, especially for old people, and with the relationship being more erratic for the younger age groups.

It is difficult to imagine that all Soviet and East European physicians give the same kind of report. The explanation might also lie in the physically weaker condition of the Soviet people due to the present inferior medical system and its failure to adapt to diseases not directly provided for in the somewhat primitive health policy. More specifically, perhaps, it may be due to the fact that the use of modern methods and structures of medicine does not necessarily produce new attitudes to health, and has, therefore, little effect on deaths caused by deeper and more long-term health factors.

This is confirmed, for instance, by the more normal levels of deaths from diseases of the circulatory system among young women. In this case, the republics seem to fit more normally into the geographical set. Indeed, the patterns for the Baltic areas relate closely to those of the Scandinavian countries, with the Ukraine in an intermediate position.

If we take into account mortality due to accidents, poisonings and other violent causes, including suicide, the distinctions appear to be different. In the case of elderly people, there is a strong positive link between the proportion of deaths from traumatisms and the proportion of deaths from neoplasms. So far as the relationship between mortality from diseases of the circulatory system and mortality from traumatisms is concerned, geographical continuity is quite marked in the younger age groups, with the Baltic republics again closely resembling the Scandinavian countries. The other republics appear to show the same linear relationship as other countries, but with higher mortality due to diseases of the circulatory system.

The last factor, which is most crucial, is the proportion of deaths due to diseases of the respiratory system. It clearly separates Central Asia from the other parts of the Union, the Transcaucasian republics being in an intermediate position. This is hardly surprising given that Central Asia has structures typical of developing countries and, indeed, is geographically contiguous to some of them. The contention that there has been no great convergence between the main trends in mortality structures in Central Asia and the European model would appear to have been proven. It would appear also to have been established that a unified health system has not had any strong effects on overall health behaviour other than in respect of some causes. Thus, Soviet medicine has not interacted with the lifestyle of the population.

This very rapid overview has already yielded some interesting indicators. The most discriminant factor appears to be, among the elderly, the proportion of deaths from diseases of the circulatory system relative to the proportion of deaths from neoplasms. It therefore highlights the contrasts between mortality due to more traditional and long-term lifestyle patterns and mortality associated with new patterns. The author is of the view that it also expresses the weak interaction between the health system and individuals; other observations make for similar conclusions. This will be referred to again at a later stage.

DOES CENTRAL ASIA EXHIBIT LDC AGE–MORTALITY PATTERNS?

The second important question raised by the mortality data is the place of the Central Asian republics in comparison with the Less Developed Countries, since it is now customary to compare that part of the USSR with the LDCs. The structure of the economic links of Central Asia with Russia, for example, is often compared to the links between developing and developed countries. It is, however, more difficult to measure the precise impact of a different structure of political links, and of the very special position of these regions inside a large country, and not separate from it. Thus, mortality according to age would seem to be a good starting point for solving this question.

In order to study this question, the author has attempted to adjust a set of life tables for LDCS (with regional patterns) to the observed life tables of the four republics of Uzbekistan, Tajikistan, Turkmenistan and Kirghizia. Kazakhstan was not included, as that republic is populated by almost equal numbers of Russians and other non-indigenous nationalities and Kazakh. The United Nations' set of life tables with certain adjustments was chosen.[6] It should be remembered that this set is based on the regional patterns of Latin America, Chile, Southern Asia and the Far East. The basic principle lies in computing the differences between the mortality rates observed in the country being studied and the mortality rates of the mean profile of a given regional pattern. These differences are then adjusted to the first and second components of a principal component analysis. The corresponding coordinates are given in the presentation of this set of life tables; the adjustment is made using the OLS method.[7]

The first results of the analysis are presented in Table 4.1; it represents the ratio of the observed mortality rates at different ages and the predicted mortality rates computed for the different sets of life tables (the four regions and the general region). These results show a clear similarity in the deviations in the younger age groups between the patterns for the different republics and the regional sets of life tables which are the most appropriate for describing such patterns (that is, the Far East, Southern Asia and the general). The deviations are the same and are characterised by an excess mortality at ages after infant mortality. It is difficult to give a precise explanation for this peak, but the first and most likely one is probably that of an underestimation of infant mortality. In the same way, the apparent decrease of the peak after age 1 could also be explained by an overestimation of mortality at age 1, due to a change of declaration of age of death for children dying before the first year (see Table 4.2)

As was noted in a previous paper,[8] it is possible that following a campaign against infant mortality physicians have been declaring children who have died before age 1 as having died at age 1. Although this statistical convention is known in other countries, it still cannot explain such a degree of deviation. Another explanation, perhaps more appropriate and interesting, might relate to infant protection which is most effective at the time of birth, when the mother is in a clinic or hospital, but which decreases greatly thereafter. It would, therefore, be an expression of the deep discrepancy

Table 4.1 Ratio of mortality rates observed/adjusted all ages

Republic	Turkmenistan										Uzbekistan									
Sex	Males					Females					Males					Females				
pattern*	LA	CH	SA	FE	G	LA	CH	SA	FE	G	LA	CH	SA	FE	G	LA	CH	SA	FE	G
Age																				
0	0.82	0.55	0.80	0.76	0.75	0.81	0.54	0.74	0.33	0.30	0.90	0.61	0.88	0.83	0.83	0.88	0.59	0.80	0.35	0.31
1	1.30	1.67	1.19	1.25	1.31	1.36	2.03	1.23	4.46	5.20	1.12	1.44	1.03	1.08	1.13	1.15	1.72	1.04	3.80	4.43
5	0.50	0.89	0.35	0.85	0.59	0.54	0.94	0.42	0.43	0.76	0.68	1.22	0.48	1.17	0.80	0.62	1.08	0.49	0.50	0.88
10	0.63	0.82	0.58	0.77	0.67	0.85	0.98	0.84	0.21	0.27	0.92	1.20	0.84	1.13	0.98	0.92	1.05	0.91	0.22	0.29
15	0.92	1.07	0.95	1.21	1.00	0.89	0.82	0.84	0.84	0.82	0.83	0.96	0.86	1.08	0.89	0.96	0.89	0.91	0.91	0.89
20	0.86	0.92	1.25	0.99	0.93	1.26	1.15	1.35	2.81	2.77	0.76	0.81	1.11	0.88	0.83	1.24	1.13	1.32	2.75	2.71
25	0.92	0.88	1.32	1.02	1.00	1.13	1.04	1.36	2.34	2.15	0.92	0.88	1.31	1.01	1.00	1.09	1.00	1.31	2.26	2.08
30	1.08	0.91	1.45	1.08	1.11	0.98	0.89	1.23	1.60	1.44	1.04	0.87	1.39	1.04	1.06	1.00	0.91	1.25	1.64	1.47
35	1.12	0.92	1.36	1.02	1.10	0.89	0.81	1.15	0.93	0.79	1.19	0.97	1.45	1.08	1.17	1.01	0.92	1.31	1.05	0.90
40	1.22	0.98	1.27	1.01	1.15	0.95	0.84	1.15	0.53	0.44	1.20	0.96	1.25	0.99	1.13	0.97	0.86	1.18	0.54	0.45
45	1.39	1.13	1.29	1.09	1.27	1.09	0.94	1.20	0.51	0.41	1.24	1.01	1.15	0.98	1.13	1.03	0.89	1.13	0.48	0.39
50	1.42	1.16	1.14	1.01	1.24	1.23	1.06	1.13	0.66	0.54	1.30	1.06	1.04	0.92	1.13	1.12	0.97	1.03	0.60	0.49
55	1.51	1.26	1.19	1.10	1.32	1.31	1.14	1.08	1.05	0.88	1.26	1.06	0.99	0.92	1.10	1.15	1.00	0.94	0.92	0.77
60	1.56	1.28	1.15	1.03	1.30	1.29	1.14	0.99	1.52	1.32	1.31	1.07	0.96	0.86	1.09	1.27	1.13	0.98	1.50	1.30
65	1.39	1.19	1.05	0.96	1.18	1.18	1.07	0.90	2.41	2.31	1.19	1.02	0.90	0.82	1.01	0.96	0.87	0.74	1.96	1.88

Republic	Tajikistan										Kirghizia									
Sex	Males					Females					Males					Females				
pattern*	LA	CH	SA	FE	G	LA	CH	SA	FE	G	LA	CH	SA	FE	G	LA	CH	SA	FE	G
Age
0	0.81	0.54	0.79	0.74	0.74	0.79	0.53	0.72	0.32	0.28	0.80	0.54	0.78	0.74	0.74	0.73	0.49	0.67	0.30	0.27
1	1.18	1.52	1.09	1.14	1.20	1.30	1.94	1.18	4.28	5.00	1.23	1.59	1.13	1.19	1.25	1.29	1.93	1.17	4.25	4.96
5	0.55	0.99	0.39	0.95	0.66	0.63	1.10	0.50	0.51	0.89	0.72	1.30	0.51	1.24	0.86	0.61	1.07	0.48	0.49	0.86
10	0.83	1.09	0.76	1.02	0.89	0.95	1.08	0.93	0.23	0.30	1.02	1.34	0.94	1.26	1.09	0.78	0.90	0.77	0.19	0.25
15	0.69	0.80	0.71	0.90	0.75	0.84	0.78	0.79	0.79	0.78	0.93	1.08	0.96	1.22	1.00	0.91	0.84	0.86	0.86	0.84
20	0.86	0.91	1.25	0.98	0.93	1.06	0.97	1.14	2.37	2.34	0.84	0.89	1.22	0.96	0.91	1.32	1.20	1.41	2.93	2.89
25	1.02	0.97	1.45	1.12	1.10	1.04	0.95	1.25	2.15	1.98	0.94	0.90	1.34	1.03	1.02	1.18	1.09	1.42	2.44	2.25
30	1.10	0.92	1.47	1.10	1.12	0.93	0.85	1.17	1.53	1.37	1.03	0.86	1.37	1.03	1.05	1.08	0.98	1.35	1.76	1.58
35	1.24	1.02	1.51	1.13	1.22	1.05	0.96	1.36	1.09	0.93	1.00	0.82	1.22	0.92	0.99	1.14	1.05	1.48	1.19	1.02
40	1.37	1.10	1.43	1.14	1.30	1.11	0.98	1.35	0.62	0.51	1.07	0.86	1.11	0.88	1.01	1.12	0.98	1.35	0.62	0.51
45	1.37	1.12	1.27	1.08	1.25	1.11	0.96	1.22	0.51	0.42	1.19	0.97	1.11	0.94	1.09	1.02	0.88	1.12	0.47	0.39
50	1.33	1.09	1.07	0.95	1.16	1.18	1.02	1.09	0.63	0.52	1.19	0.98	0.96	0.85	1.04	1.06	0.92	0.97	0.57	0.46
55	1.25	1.04	0.98	0.90	1.08	1.15	1.00	0.94	0.92	0.77	1.15	0.96	0.90	0.83	1.00	1.06	0.93	0.87	0.85	0.72
60	1.27	1.05	0.94	0.83	1.06	1.42	1.26	1.09	1.67	1.45	1.18	0.96	0.86	0.77	0.98	1.07	0.95	0.82	1.27	1.10
65	1.32	1.13	1.00	0.91	1.12	1.06	0.96	0.81	2.16	2.07	1.21	1.03	0.91	0.83	1.02	0.90	0.82	0.69	1.84	1.76

* Mortality patterns: LA = Latin American, CH = Chilean, FA = Far Eastern, SA = South Asian, G = General.

Sources: Based upon 'Model life tables for developing countries', *Population Studies*, vol. 77 (1982); and *Naselenie SSSR 1988* (Moscow: Finansy i statistika, 1989).

Table 4.2   Number of births (per 10 000) and infant mortality rate
(deaths per 1000), 1950–1987

Year	IMR	Births
1950	80.7	480
1951	83.7	495
1952	74.8	495
1953	67.6	475
1954	68.2	513
1955	59.6	505
1956	47.4	502
1957	45.3	516
1958	40.6	524
1959	40.6	526
1960	35.3	534
1961	32.3	519
1962	32.2	496
1963	30.9	476
1964	28.8	446
1965	27.2	425
1966	26.1	424
1967	26.0	409
1968	26.4	409
1969	25.8	409
1970	24.7	422
1971	22.9	437
1972	24.7	440
1973	26.4	439
1974	27.9	455
1975	30.6	461
1976	31.4	472
1977	30.5	469
1978	29.2	476
1979	27.4	481
1980	27.3	485
1981	26.9	496
1982	25.7	510
1983	25.3	539
1984	25.9	539
1985	26.0	537
1986	25.4	561
1987	25.4	560

Source: as Table 4.1.

between a health policy based on the importation of medical practices tending to concentrate on the problems of the deaths of children at birth, and a population that has not yet adopted good child care habits. It is also a further example of the gap between political measures and their interaction with the population. It is relatively easy in a centrally planned health system to protect young children against infectious diseases or birth traumas, but such a system is not conducive to effective long-term child care.

Such an explanation has, therefore, profound consequences for overall mortality trends in the Soviet Union. Indeed, it is well-known that the USSR experienced a very sharp decline in infant mortality just before and after World War II, falling in the 1950s to forty deaths per thousand. Even if the reality of such a decline is difficult to assess, it is nevertheless easy to see that a voluntary policy based on a great number of vaccination campaigns and the development of small medical units can readily produce such a decrease. It does not, however, work a deeper transformation and leads, on the contrary, to people being more prone to illness; this might well explain not only the increase in infant mortality at age 1 but also adult mortality. Therefore, one element of explanation of the increase in adult mortality, which would appear not to contradict the Anderson and Silver cohort analysis, could well be this paradoxical association with a sharp decline in infant mortality.

More provocatively, perhaps, the author suggests that infant mortality declined too sharply in the 1950s, and that the rigid, centrally-planned health system was unable to adapt itself to a changed, more modern situation. Another argument in this direction relates to the problem of the increase in infant mortality of the 1970s, the subject of a thorough study by Davies and Feshbach many years ago.[9] A Soviet scholar has recently pointed out the parallel between this increase, the date of the beginning of the deterioration, and the change in the trend in the absolute numbers of births.[10] In fact, if the system were incapable of adapting to an increase in the absolute numbers of births, this might well be seen as proof of its unwieldiness and of the non-adaptation of the population.

Beyond the younger age groups adjustment is less coherent, and would seem to be expressive of some distortion between infant and adult mortality, as compared with other developing countries. In order to eliminate such distortions, we have based our estimations on more suitable tables, using only mortality for age fifteen years and over. We have, therefore, used only the first component of analysis (Table 4.3).

Table 4.3 Ratio of mortality rates observed/adjusted ages from 15 (one component)

Republic	Turkmenistan										Uzbekistan									
Sex	Males					Females					Males					Females				
pattern*	AL	CH	SA	FE	G	AL	CH	SA	FE	G	AL	CH	SA	FE	G	AL	CH	SA	FE	G
Age
15	0.75	0.93	0.78	0.94	0.80	0.82	0.87	0.71	0.68	0.79	0.77	0.96	0.80	0.96	0.81	0.89	0.95	0.77	0.74	0.86
20	0.73	0.89	0.97	0.95	0.82	1.13	1.18	1.15	2.06	2.31	0.71	0.87	0.94	0.92	0.80	1.14	1.19	1.16	2.07	2.32
25	0.80	0.89	1.01	1.03	0.91	1.02	1.07	1.16	1.77	1.85	0.86	0.96	1.09	1.11	0.98	1.01	1.05	1.15	1.74	1.82
30	0.95	0.94	1.10	1.15	1.03	0.92	0.95	1.06	1.40	1.48	0.97	0.97	1.13	1.18	1.06	0.93	0.97	1.08	1.43	1.51
35	0.99	0.95	1.05	1.08	1.03	0.85	0.88	1.01	0.86	0.86	1.12	1.08	1.19	1.23	1.17	0.95	0.98	1.13	0.96	0.96
40	1.08	0.98	1.02	1.01	1.06	0.92	0.90	1.03	0.51	0.48	1.13	1.03	1.08	1.06	1.11	0.92	0.90	1.04	0.51	0.48
45	1.23	1.10	1.08	1.04	1.15	1.03	0.97	1.09	0.45	0.40	1.18	1.05	1.03	1.00	1.10	0.98	0.92	1.03	0.43	0.38
50	1.27	1.11	0.99	0.93	1.12	1.16	1.08	1.04	0.56	0.49	1.24	1.08	0.97	0.90	1.09	1.07	0.99	0.96	0.52	0.45
55	1.37	1.20	1.07	0.99	1.19	1.22	1.12	1.00	0.83	0.72	1.22	1.06	0.95	0.88	1.06	1.10	1.01	0.90	0.75	0.65
60	1.44	1.23	1.06	0.95	1.20	1.20	1.12	0.93	1.21	1.08	1.27	1.08	0.93	0.83	1.06	1.23	1.14	0.95	1.23	1.10
65	1.29	1.13	0.98	0.87	1.08	1.08	1.00	0.86	1.65	1.52	1.16	1.01	0.88	0.78	0.97	0.93	0.86	0.74	1.43	1.32

Republic	Tajikistan										Kirghizia									
Sex	Males					Females					Males					Females				
pattern*	AL	CH	SA	FE	G	AL	CH	SA	FE	G	AL	CH	SA	FE	G	AL	CH	SA	FE	G
Age
15	0.62	0.77	0.64	0.78	0.66	0.79	0.84	0.69	0.66	0.76	0.83	1.03	0.86	1.04	0.88	0.82	0.88	0.72	0.69	0.80
20	0.76	0.92	1.00	0.98	0.85	1.00	1.04	1.01	1.81	2.03	0.81	0.99	1.07	1.04	0.91	1.17	1.22	1.18	2.12	2.38
25	0.90	1.00	1.14	1.16	1.02	0.98	1.02	1.11	1.68	1.76	0.93	1.04	1.18	1.20	1.06	1.06	1.10	1.20	1.82	1.91
30	0.96	0.96	1.12	1.17	1.04	0.88	0.92	1.02	1.35	1.43	1.03	1.03	1.20	1.26	1.12	1.00	1.03	1.15	1.53	1.61
35	1.10	1.06	1.17	1.20	1.15	1.00	1.04	1.19	1.01	1.01	1.01	0.97	1.08	1.11	1.06	1.08	1.12	1.29	1.09	1.09
40	1.24	1.12	1.18	1.15	1.21	1.07	1.05	1.20	0.59	0.56	1.05	0.96	1.00	0.98	1.03	1.07	1.04	1.20	0.59	0.56
45	1.26	1.12	1.10	1.06	1.17	1.07	1.01	1.12	0.46	0.41	1.16	1.03	1.01	0.98	1.08	0.96	0.91	1.01	0.42	0.37
50	1.24	1.09	0.97	0.91	1.09	1.14	1.06	1.02	0.55	0.48	1.14	1.00	0.89	0.83	1.00	1.00	0.92	0.89	0.48	0.42
55	1.18	1.03	0.92	0.85	1.03	1.11	1.02	0.91	0.75	0.65	1.09	0.95	0.85	0.79	0.95	0.99	0.91	0.81	0.67	0.58
60	1.21	1.04	0.89	0.80	1.01	1.37	1.28	1.06	1.38	1.23	1.13	0.96	0.82	0.74	0.94	1.00	0.93	0.77	1.01	0.89
65	1.27	1.11	0.96	0.86	1.07	1.02	0.95	0.82	1.57	1.45	1.16	1.01	0.87	0.78	0.97	0.82	0.76	0.65	1.25	1.16

* Mortality patterns: LA = Latin American, CH = Chilean, FA = Far Eastern, SA = South Asian, G= General

Source: as Table 4.1

The results, again, are consistent, and express a regularity in the discrepancy between the theory and the observed tables. The more important discrepancies are due to higher mortality at ages 20 to 50 years, and can be explained by reference to the mortality patterns of more developed countries, with increased mortality due to accidents. It might also be explained in part by mortality among Russians and other non-indigenes living in these republics and the native Kazakh, although the differences between republics can hardly be understood by mere reference to a differential based on the presence of immigrants. It is probably, therefore, also the consequence of a weakened population, which although surviving infant death is not attuned to modern medical practices. Again, the peak is more marked for females than males. However, the second peak for females can only be explained as a problem of the declaration of age, with a bias to age 60 years.

Such conclusions are confirmed by an analysis of the maternal mortality levels derived from the life tables.[11] The level appears to be characteristic of that of developing countries, even if not so high. The decrease would appear to be less marked for the main republic of Central Asia (Uzbekistan), and might also be a reflection of the stagnating effects of the system.

The strong sensitivity of adult mortality was highlighted by the initial effects of the 1985 anti-alcohol legislation (mortality at ages 20–30 years decreased by 20 per cent within a year). Another example of this sensitivity can be found in the strong correlation between mortality due to suicide, and the application of the 'dry laws'. Thus, the number of suicides per 100 000 of the population fell from 82 in 1984 to 53 in 1986, and rose again to 56 in 1988 when the legislation ceased to be applied.[12]

These observations lead one to the conclusion that the demographic structures of Central Asia, if they approximate to those seen in the life tables of the LDCs, are also marked by the growth of new mortality patterns which have not yet suppressed the old ones. It is yet another indication of the incapacity of the health system to adapt to new mortality structures and, at the same time, to serve to maintain existing forms of health protection while adapting to real changes in sanitary and medical habits. At a conference in Paris the Soviet demographer A. Vishnevsky[13] pointed to the difficulty of changing health habits by direct government action; the evidence we have considered amply bears out this observation.

CONCLUSION

This study permits us to draw important conclusions about the overall structure of a health policy and the links existing between the actual mortality trends and the health standards of a given population. In the first place it shows that if a strictly centrally planned policy can easily lead to a decrease in the most prominent and evident causes of death, it also creates a very fragile situation and in some respects a deterioration. Nor does it solve the problem of the discrepancy caused by the gap between the technical measures of an imported system hastily put in place and its deep integration into the social and cultural structure, which includes popular health practices. As a recent book on the technical aspects of Soviet medicine has noted,[14] there is a tendency to early specialisation in medical training, leading in turn to a dearth of general practitioners. The perception of medicine that was popular in the Stalin years, as consisting primarily of techniques, meant that better practices failed to become widely accepted by the population at large. The present analysis has shown up the truth of this in considerable relief.

This analysis also poses the question of the capacity of the system to adapt to the fundamental differences in the Soviet regions. The Soviet health system has, certainly, not succeeded in changing the native patterns of these regions, but has been the mere accompaniment of decline, and has even resulted in instability, where changes have been quite artificial. A quick comparison of fertility trends in Central Asia shows that the decline is to be explained not in the context of the USSR but of that of other culturally close countries (Azerbaijan displays similar trends to those of Turkey, and Uzbekistan is apparently comparable to Iran). The lack of a connection between long-term trends and political structures is reflected once more in the study of mortality. It raises, in fact, the question as to whether the direction of an evolutionary path can be changed, where the means used are not adapted to very specific local conditions. It is the conviction of the author that such 'paths' have great consequences for the health policies of the developing countries, and that a more intensive study of them would be useful for creating policies not specifically orientated to current European conditions.

Notes

1. B. A. Anderson and B. Silver, 'Patterns of cohort mortality in the Soviet Union', *Population and Development Review*, no. 15, 3 September 1989.

2. Alain Blum and Alain Monnier, 'Recent mortality trends in the USSR: new evidence', *Population Studies*, vol. 43 (1989), pp. 211–41; and Alain Blum and Alain Monnier, 'La mortalité selon la cause en Union Soviétique', *Population*, vol. 44 (1989), pp. 1053-1100.
3. *Naselenie SSSR 1988* (Moscow: Finansy i statistika, 1989).
4. Blum and Monnier, 'Recent mortality trends'.
5. Ibid.
6. 'Model life tables for developing countries', *Population Studies*, vol. 77 (United Nations Organization, New York, 1982).
7. I have used the second component because it contains infant mortality differentials. The use of only the first component did not take sufficient account of the variability of this mortality category.
8. A. Blum and R. Pressat, 'Une nouvelle table de mortalité pour l'URSS (1984–1985)', *Population*, no. 6, 1987, pp. 843–62.
9. C. Davies and M. Feshbach, 'Rising infant mortality in the Soviet Union in the 1970s', US Bureau of the Census, Series P, 1980.
10. L. Rybakovsky at the INED Conference, Paris, December 1989.
11. The methodology of estimating maternal mortality based on life tables is presented in A. Blum and P. Fargues, 'Rapid estimations of maternal mortality in countries with defective data', *Population Studies*, no. 44, 1990, pp. 155–71. (Observed female mortality rates are estimated without taking account of maternal mortality and on the basis of three methods. The curve, with a break around 40 years, represents the observed maternal mortality rates, while the other more regular curves represent an estimate of female mortality without including maternal deaths.)
12. See the figures contained in ibid.
13. INED Conference, Paris, April 1989.
14. Michael Ryan, *Doctors and the State in the Soviet Union* (London: Macmillan, 1989).

5 The Battle Continues: Gorbachev's Anti-Alcoholism Policies

Walter Joyce

The call 'Alcoholism and socialism are incompatible!' has resounded on and off throughout the years of Soviet power. Public policy during these years has aimed at nothing less than the resolution of what is held to be 'one of the most difficult tasks of the cultural revolution . . . the transformation of the social consciousness of wide sections of the population and the whole structure of their spiritual life and morals'.[1] More specifically government policy has been conducted in terms of a struggle against any 'survivals and birthmarks of capitalism in the minds and conduct of the people', starting with the 'struggle against drunkenness as the very basis of almost all of the negative phenomena in society, at work and in the family'. Under socialism, it is held, drunkenness and alcoholism, even when they have become residual, remain complex social factors, the elimination of which lies in the sphere of economic, moral–legal, and preventive–medical education. The struggle against alcohol, accordingly, is an inseparable part of communist education, because socialism and drunkenness, and even more communism and drunkenness, are seen as incompatible.[2]

However, while holding fast to the principle of sobriety, the Soviet state has too often shown an uncertain resolve, ensuring that the fate of successive anti-alcohol drives has been much dependent upon the particular economic or social priorities of the moment. The consequence has been to cast serious doubt on the intentions of the state and party in the minds of the advocates of sobriety, and equally to reassure its opponents. Thus, the infant Russian republic in November 1917 took steps to re-establish 'strict revolutionary order and to suppress attempts at anarchy on the part of drunks and hooligans'.[3] This was followed in 1918, due to a temporary loss of the Caucasus oil fields, by the decision to begin the production of alcohol as a fuel substitute. In December 1919 a decree of the RSFSR, while forbidding the production and sale of alcohol on its territory, did not entirely prohibit the consumption of alcohol but aimed principally at the protection of grain supplies. In the middle of 1920, 953 alcohol plants were nationalised with all of the production going for industrial purposes; the production of spirit for personal consumption was forbidden.[4] The picture was further complicated by the differences in prices of industrial and agricultural commodities, a factor persuading peasants to divert grain supplies away from the market to the more profitable sphere of illicit distilling. However, the resultant 500 000 or so prosecutions for that offence in 1922 were conducted with uncharacteristic leniency for the times, being put down to 'cultural backwardness' and drawing only fines and warnings.

Due to the acute need for additional sources of domestic accumulation, it was decided in August 1925 to permit the sale of vodka, and the monopoly of its production was allocated to Gosspirt VSNKh (State Alcohol Authority, Higher Council of the National Economy). This was conceived as a temporary measure designed to bring in additional revenues for investment in the country's industrialisation. It was assumed that, in time, other more acceptable sources of investment would be found, once more allowing the production of alcohol by the state to be ended.

As it happened, per capita levels of alcohol consumption for the period to 1927 were little above those of the immediate pre-war years (in 1913 per capita consumption was 8.6 litres, whereas in 1927 it was 8.7 litres). However, concern was focused upon the consequences of alcohol abuse: in 1927 losses due to alcohol-related absenteeism led to a decrease in labour productivity amounting to 135 million roubles and 600 million roubles respectively.[5]

The XV Congress of the CPSU in 1927 formally recognised that the struggle against alcoholism could only be successfully waged with the participation of state, party, soviet and social organisations. A lengthy anti-alcohol campaign ensued in the press. In September 1926 a resolution of the Council of People's Commissars of the RSFSR had emphasised measures of prevention and educational propaganda, and the RSFSR People's Commissariat for Health was charged with intensifying its study of prevention and treatment of alcoholism through a network of neuro-psychiatric institutions. Finally, the Commissariats for Health, Justice and the NKVD were directed to take part in a wide range of propaganda and educational activities.[6]

In February 1928 a meeting of anti-alcohol 'enthusiasts' formed itself into the 'Society for the Struggle Against Alcoholism' (OBSA), and later in the same year began publication of its journal *Trezvost' i kul'tura* (Sobriety and Culture). Throughout the period 1928–32 the Society concentrated its attention on the promotion of measures for restricting the production and sale of alcohol, the struggle against illicit distilling and speculation, anti-alcohol propaganda and education, and giving help to alcoholism sufferers. In June 1928, for example, the Society prepared a draft decree for the consideration of the Council of People's Commissars, proposing the gradual reduction in the production of alcoholic beverages to nil, the complete elimination of illicit distilling, increased production of non-alcoholic beverages, the strategic location and, where necessary, closure of alcohol-retail points, strict age limits on the purchase of alcohol, social–cultural and educational measures and, finally, increased legal sanctions on abusers.[7]

At the beginning of the 1930s this broad front against alcohol and its abuse was radically reversed. The order was given to switch from 'narrow anti-alcohol work' to an all-out struggle for improvements in the conditions of everyday life. It was now explained that a resolution of the problems of drunkenness and alcoholism depended on the improved wellbeing of the people, 'inasmuch as under socialism such bourgeois survivals cannot flourish'.[8] In 1930 the RSFSR Anti-Alcohol Society was abolished, and in 1932 all of the Societies for the Struggle Against Alcoholism were merged with the 'Union of the Godless' and the 'Down With Illiteracy' society, and the resultant hybrid became known as the 'Society for a Healthy Life'.

Not only did the medical opinion on alcohol alter, allowing for it at times to be used as a medicine, but it disappeared from the central and local press as an issue. In 1930 even the statistical materials on the production and sale of alcohol and its social and other consequences ceased to be published. This latter fact served to conceal until only recently the degree to which local and central administrations had become dependent upon alcohol revenues.[9] The period of the Second World War concentrated minds and energies elsewhere, and it was not until the 1950s that formal attention was drawn once more to the struggle against alcohol abuse.

In 1958 a decree of the Central Committee of the CPSU and the USSR Council of Ministers 'On the Intensification of the Struggle Against Drunkenness and the Reduction in the Sales of Alcoholic Beverages' was followed by a resolution of the USSR Ministry of Health in the same year, 'On the Means of the Prevention and Treatment of Alcoholism', which recommended the creation of alcoholism units in psycho-neurological clinics and within the other branches of the health service, especially in industrial premises. Later, in 1977, all union and republican Commissions for the Struggle against Alcoholism were set up. In 1977 decrees of the Central Committee of the CPSU and the USSR Council of Ministers' 'On Perfecting Health Care' put the emphasis on combating alcohol abuse through the medium of health education. Successive sallies against alcohol abuse in the late 1970s and early 1980s, in the form of increased prices of alcohol and more severe punishments for violations of the existing anti-alcohol legislation, failed to stem the rising tide of consumption, and the consequent impact on Soviet society was of unprecedentedly high mortality levels, greatly increased incidence of drink-related illness and absenteeism, disorders and inefficiency in the workplace, and domestic problems. Unfortunately, only limited and approximate (inferential) evaluations of alcohol-consumption statistics for the period up to the mid-1980s are possible, as 'moral' statistics (on alcoholism, prostitution, drug abuse, and so on) largely ceased to be made public in 1934 with the abolition of the Department of Moral Statistics, and, with the brief exception of the year 1962, did not begin to become available again until the latter half of the 1980s. However, it has been calculated by Treml[10] that 'between 1960 and the mid-1980s consumption more than doubled, reaching a level of 15.16 litres of absolute alcohol per person 15 years of age and older'.

Finally in 1985, in the spirit of radical renewal of that year, it was decided that the age-old scourge of alcohol abuse should be expunged once and for all from the face of Soviet society. Towards this end a decree of the Presidium of the USSR Supreme Soviet was published on 16 May 1985, 'On the Intensification of the Struggle against Drunkenness', which resolved, in addition, upon 'a decisive stop to illicit distilling, and the greater strengthening of social order and labour discipline'.[11] The sanctions decreed included fines of 20–30 roubles for the consumption of alcohol in most public places or for appearing in a public place in a state of intoxication. In addition, any repetition of such offences within a year after having been given an administrative reprimand would render the offender liable to a further fine of 30–40 roubles. Appearing in the workplace in a state of intoxication, or any failure on the part of supervisors to check such conduct, would incur similar penalties. Sanctions such as corrective labour or much larger fines awaited those who involved themselves in illicit distilling or speculation in alcohol. Abetting the consumption of alcohol by under-age persons (that is, under 21 years) would also incur fines. Significantly enough, then, in the new anti-alcohol drive the first resort was to legal sanctions.

THE WAYS AND THE MEANS

The extensive press coverage which accompanied the introduction of the anti-alcohol drive emphasised the all-embracing character of the drive, in contrast to all previous attempts which were dismissed as mere 'campaigns' of short duration. Thus, in addition to the legal sanctions outlined above, the 'drive' also involved reduced hours of opening of alcohol retail points and a reduction in the actual number of the latter, increased prices (from 1986), and an end to the production of fruit-and berry-based fortified wines (*bormotukha*) by 1988. In addition, recidivists would find themselves increasingly likely to end up in LTPs (Treatment-Labour Prophylacteries) which were patterned after labour colonies. It was also decided to expand leisure facilities, such as extra equipment and premises for sport and physical culture, non-alcohol cafes and bars, increased treatment facilities for alcoholics, and the activisation of education and propaganda of the healthy way of life. In addition, an All-Union Society for the Struggle for Sobriety, the successor to the old 'Society for the Struggle Against Alcoholism', was formed and the journal *Sobriety and Culture* was resurrected in 1986.

Successive decrees and resolutions followed the gradual construction of a grand superstructure of exhortation, compulsion and persuasion. Thus, on 16 June 1985, the Central Committee of the CPSU passed a decree 'On Measures for Improving the Use of Clubs and Sporting Equipment'.[12] The decree noted the lack of such facilities as sports and hobbies clubs, houses of culture, the often scarce and delapidated condition of the existing facilities, and the vital importance these had for 'ideological-moral education, propaganda of the Soviet way of life, the unmasking of bourgeois ideology and morals, the overcoming of consumer psychology, religious survivals, and the struggle against drunkenness and other anti-social phenomena'. Every ministry, state committee, and social organisation was enlisted to carry out a wide-ranging inventory of existing sporting and cultural facilities and services, and a number were directed to report back to the USSR Council of Ministers by 1 January 1986 with their proposals for greatly expanding the range. In addition plans were made to set aside more land for garden plots, increase the availability of car and motor-cycle spares, photographic and artists' materials; in all, anything which would divert resources and energies away from the consumption of alcohol.

In September 1985, the Central Committee of the CPSU reviewed the course of the implementation of the decree 'On Measures for Overcoming Drunkenness and Alcoholism'. While welcoming the universal approval of every section of Soviet society for the new anti-alcohol measures, a special plea for party members to give a proper example was followed by a warning that abusers could find themselves expelled from the party.[13] Notice was given of the impending publication of *Sobriety and Culture*, the journal of the newly-established sobriety society, and note was made of the slight increase in the availability of non-alcoholic beverages and of the need for more consumer goods. The sharpening struggle against speculation in alcoholic beverages and illicit distilling was welcomed, one token of which was that 'a large number of stills had been put out of action, and that a substantial number had been surrendered voluntarily'. However, it was added that 'a certain section of that part of the population given to drinking disapproved of and awaited a weakening of the measures directed against drunkenness'.

As noted above, 1985 also saw the old 'Society for the Struggle Against Alcoholism' revived with the more positive title of 'All-Union Society for the Struggle for Sobriety', and also revived was its journal, *Sobriety and Culture*. The Society was to function, in addition to the 55 000 communists who were organised to assist the police to enforce the anti-alcohol laws in the streets,[14] as the shock-troops of the anti-alcohol drive. Their function was to propagandise in favour of total abstinence and to run treatment and rehabilitation schemes. The Society, although with a broad membership of unpaid volunteers, was to have a professional, full-time staff. By the end of 1989 the Society numbered almost 13 million members: three and a half million of them were under 30 years of age and 4.7 million were industrial and collective farm workers. The members were organised in some 394 227 primary organisations. In the same year the estimated income of the Society was 15.5 million roubles, 70 per cent from membership dues, 5 per cent from sales of publications, 5 per cent from donations from the earnings of its organisations, and 18 per cent in subsidies from the official trade unions (VTsSPS). Currently, most of the resources go to propaganda work, membership badges and cards, lectures, and subscriptions to journals.[15] The Society trains its psychotherapists according to the

'Dovzhenko' method of breaking alcohol-dependence and the Shich-ko 'psychological and pedagogical methods of influencing the human personality' (see below). Unfortunately for the reputation of the Society, almost from the first the growth of its apparatus outstripped that of the membership. Complaints were made of bureaucratism, formalism, and downright opportunism. The editorial board of *Sobriety and Culture* itself insisted that for a time after the Society was formed a 'natural selection' of activists had ensured the worthy replenishment of its ranks: 'The best of them are real fighters for sobriety and *perestroika* and who adhere in practice to the values of socialism, cleansed of the rust of distortions of the Stalin era and of the period of stagnation'.[16] However, admission was also made that the 1985 Constituent Conference of the Society had a fairly massive representation of 'indifferent bureaucrats', 'lazy windbags', all 'avoiding the dirty work and covering up', so that 'We paid for it with four years of initiatives and mistakes, and at no little cost to the authority of the Society, the ideas of sobriety in general, and the sobriety platform which had been laid down by the Central Committee of the CPSU in May 1985'.[17]

The concern of the party for the parlous condition of the Society was expressed in a decree of the Central Committee of the CPSU on 26 October 1989 'On the Restructuring of the Work of the All-Union Voluntary Society for the Struggle for Sobriety'.[18] While calling for the Society to be supported by all organisations of state and society, the decree dwelt on the need to eliminate 'formalism and breaches of the voluntary principle in admissions to the Society'.[19] New emphasis was put on the real self-government and the development of local initiative in organising co-operatives in the leisure and public catering spheres, working with alcohol abusers and problem families, and even consumer services to people living in remote areas.

The Society's journal, *Sobriety and Culture*, is like the Society itself in being determinedly total-abstaining in tone, and while initially somewhat Slavist-chauvinist in character it seems gradually to have shifted to a more radical position, publishing approving interviews with strike committee leaders in the Kemerovo region or radical deputies in the Congress of People's Deputies. Unfortunately, the frequent charge of anti-semitism levelled against the journal and some sections of the Society seemed in some respect to be justified by the publication of the condensed version of a very lengthy 'open letter'[20] by a certain B. I. Iskakov, which purported to be a kind of distillation of the views of the Society's members expressed in the course of a great many meetings and rallies. In essence, the letter sought to explore the origins of the anti-alcohol movement in the Soviet Union, going on to denounce the losses sustained through alcoholism, together with the activities, wittingly or unwittingly harmful, of 'moderate drinkers'. However, the letter then warned that 'If we do not want events similar to those which took place in 1964, which saw the leadership in the hands of stagnating Brezhnevism and its zionocratic clan, we have to decide upon a more resolute policy of ideological dethronement by means of cathartic propaganda and the curbing of the organisational measures of the retail-industrial-alcohol mafia and the bureaucratic alcohol lobby'.[21]

Iskakov, in passing, gave details of a number of resolutions passed at meetings and rallies of activists of the Society in Moscow, Riga, Kiev and elsewhere. The substance of Resolution number 2 demanded the fair representation of all nationalities of the USSR in all of the vitally important spheres of society, taking into account, it emphasises darkly, 'mixed marriages and artifically changed surnames, forenames and patronymics and also of the "nationality" column in documents'.[22] Somewhat more pointedly, the resolution went on to warn that should the key posts in the directing organs, the mass media, the ministries and departments and regional party and soviet organs fall into the hands of the 'eurocracy', 'then tomorrow that very eurocracy (and through it, the zionocracy), under the guise of the struggle against bureaucracy, will demand a general change of political leadership in the party and the country, and then *perestroika* and sobriety will become bogged down'.[23]

The editorial addendum to the letter made clear its general disapproval of the contents and language, and asked rhetorically how sobriety could be enhanced in society 'if alcohol addiction is to be replaced, let's say, by zionomania which is, let's be completely frank about it, just a cover for the primeval narcotic of judophobia?'[24] The editors went on to question almost every assertion in the letter, and invited the readership to comment in future numbers of the journal. A critical survey of readers' letters was published in number 7 for 1989 of the journal, and although the responses of the readers varied in character, only a few came out against the sentiments expressed in the 'open letter'. The editor declared himself unwilling to cite in detail the contents of readers' letters, since no amount of *glasnost'* could justify the propagandising of 'national difference and hostility'.[25] The prevailing tone of the letters did serve to confirm the general fixation with anti-semitism.

While it is always difficult to assess in precise terms the actual influence of such agitational organisations, anecdotal evidence suggests that 'the Society for the Struggle for Sobriety has not yet become an organisation commanding authority'.[26] It is blamed also for not finding really active forms of activity which would bring the mass of workers into its ranks. There are also complaints that it has to labour under the effects of a hostile press largely in favour of 'moderate drinking' and giving mostly one-sided and unfavourable reports on the Society.[27] Certainly, in contrast to the heady days of 1985–6, with their massive daily coverage of the anti-alcohol drive, uniformly abstentionist in tone, and generally approving of the activities of the Society, subsequent mass-circulation press treatment has fallen off dramatically and has generally been opposed to total abstinence. Little help seems forthcoming from such social organisations as the Komsomol, 'and even among party activists, the prevailing opinion is that the Society is a dead loss'.[28] The hostility of the press and much public opinion is shared by the USSR Health Ministry.[29] Recent increases in the production and sale of alcoholic beverages has apparently served to increase the mood of pessimism of a large section of the membership, and many have given up working for the Society. Formalism, rigid prohibitionist attitudes, and a general lack of initiative 'have seen the Society sustain its greatest losses in the Lithuanian SSR, the Karelian ASSR, the Primorskii *krai*, Arkhangel'sk, Perm', Pskov, Tyumen' and a number of other regions'.

Of more measurable impact is treatment, which takes two forms, voluntary and compulsory. The latter form is that of the so-called LTP (*Lechebno-trudovaya profilaktoriya*, or Treatment-Labour Prophylactory). Persistently anti-social alcoholics are sent to such institutions under the appropriate provisions of both the criminal and administrative codes. The LTP system was created some twenty years ago,[30] and in many respects the treatment regimen still resembles that of the corrective labour institutions upon which it was deliberately modelled: 'Patients' are not permitted to vote, they are subject to isolation and engage in compulsory work. The typical physical layout of the LTP is of a main building, a dining hall and an administrative block. The whole complex is surrounded by wire as in a labour camp and is guarded by units of the MVD, the latter holding joint authority with the Ministry of Health. The patients have their hair cropped, are dressed alike, 'and all have the same watchful look'.[31]

The two forms of treatment available in the LTP (although the compulsory work is itself seen as remedial) are medicinal and psychotherapeutic. The medicinal form of treatment is characterised as 'invariably accompanied by extremely unpleasant sensations, and people are afraid to go into the room where we try to produce the vomiting effect. This does not make for positive results'.[32] An additional problem is that in-patient medicinal treatment has to be completed within 25 days. The very ambiguity inherent in a system where LTPs are under the joint subordination of the MVD and the Ministry of Health, regardless of the goodwill of the staffs, is that there arises a certain conflict of choice of whether to punish or treat.[33] In addition, there is a tendency for MVD officials to lay down instructions which the medical personnel see as strictly within their own competence.[34]

More seriously, there is the problem of the often arbitrary nature of committal to an LTP, and there appear to be substantial deficiencies in the system of norms determining the rights and obligations of persons suffering from alcoholism.[35] For example, people sent for compulsory treatment are not numbered among those who have the right of recompense for any material losses sustained by them in such circumstances, which are otherwise provided for in the decree of the Praesidium of the USSR Supreme Soviet of 18 May 1981 'On the Recompense of Citizens for Any Loss Sustained as a Result of Illegal Actions on the Part of State and Social Organizations and Also by Official Persons in the Course of their Duties'.[36] However, even the policy of the USSR Health Ministry is in favour of retaining the right of compulsory treatment.[37] Attempts so far at ameliorating the more prison-like features of the system have consisted of establishing a 'staged' progress through the LTP from the 'zone', the initial and strictest regimen, with the next stage allowing separate dormitory accommodation in an experimental unit for those 'who have had the fetters of alcohol removed from them'. They are then to some degree self-sufficient in that they are given a wage for the work they do and are allowed to dispose of their free time as they see fit; the only restriction is that the 'patients' must return to spend the night in the LTP dormitory. However, those 'patients' who backslide after having been released are sent not to the dormitory but back to the zones, and so to resume the whole course of treatment all over again. The 'model' patients are encouraged gradually to seek work outside the LTP in factories located in the region. In this way, they are helped towards social and labour rehabilitation, which is otherwise an extremely difficult problem.[38]

Regardless of the continued approval of most official institutions of compulsory treatment, albeit of a more 'humane' and treatment-based form, the LTP system is very controversial. Its opponents point to a success rate of roughly only 10 per cent, when 50 per cent of those sent to LTPs have already undergone previous custodial sentences and 25 per cent have been inmates of LTPs at least once before.[39] Opponents also contend that LTPs are a breach of Articles 42 and 57 of the USSR Constitution and as such are an infringement of civil liberties; compulsory treatment they see as a 'stalinist norm' and as out-dated as psychiatric repression.[40]

The increased number of offences which were liable under the legislation introduced from 1985 – especially in respect of appearing in public in a state of intoxication – from the start imposed a heavy burden on the police 'Department for the Implementation of Anti-Alcohol Legislation and the Prevention of Drunkenness', which runs the *medtrezviteli*, or sobering-up stations, to which those who offend human dignity in such ways are taken for overnight detention and treatment and fine.[41]

Before 1986, for example, when the decision was taken to 'consolidate' them, sobering-up stations existed in every district of Moscow. In 1986 they were reduced from 33 to 11. However, the number of drunks requiring to be accommodated in them increased. By 1989, on the initiative of the MVD, their number increased once again to 21, although even then they were only able to accommodate a maximum of 540 men and 21 women at any one time.[42] Given that in 1988, 316 000 people were arrested on the streets of Moscow in a state of medium to heavy intoxication, with 144 000 ending up in sobering-up stations, it is perhaps surprising to discover that the stations are, according to the authorities, only 80 per cent occupied at any one time.[43] More disquieting, however, is the fact that although these sobering-up stations are also ostensibly medical aid stations, not one of the Moscow ones has a qualified physician on the staff (the staff are mainly medical assistants). Again, according to the authorities,[44] between 7 and 8 people die annually while in custody in the Moscow sobering-up stations, although it is insisted that the staff are not to blame.[45] Nonetheless, the provision of medical equipment and consulting rooms is very poor: in none of the capital's stations are there alcohol-measuring instruments which would permit people to be breathalysed.[46] Since, by and large, one may assume Moscow to be the best case (and this appears to be supported by other anecdotal evidence), the situation elsewhere in the former Soviet Union must surely be even worse.

In an interview in 1987 on the role of medicine in the anti-alcohol drive,[47] the Soviet Health Minister, E. I. Chazov, admitted that while initially Soviet medicine was orientated to prevention, subsequently this approach had fallen in the order of priorities. The result is that demands are made for increased in- and out-patient facilities to the detriment of developing education and propaganda in favour of sobriety. The present standard of pamphlets and textbooks on addictions and related issues, the Minister admitted, was 'poor'. An additional need, he continued, was for health centres, where people could pursue common interests, as an alternative to sports stadiums which did not appeal to everyone. It was Chazov's view that the problem of how to deal with the large number of alcoholics was more social than medical. However, the Health Ministry was constantly reviewing the standard of narcological services, including the attestation of the quality of medical personnel, and making any necessary changes in the organisation of treatment facilities.

The generally optimistic tone of the interview was not seen to have been entirely justified two years later, when the state provision of narcological services was reviewed by senior officials of the People's Control Commission of the USSR.[48] It was stated that while the state network of narcological services was funded to the tune of 500 million roubles annually, the work was generally of poor quality. It was observed that 'The material base of the narcological institutions and sub-departments is being consolidated only slowly, and it is not sufficient to provide full medical help'. It was found that substantial numbers of alcoholism sufferers had fallen outside the field of view of medical workers, as a result of which they were deprived of treatment and rehabilitation measures which would have allowed them to resume full-time employment. The RSFSR Public Health Ministry, for example, reported that it had taken appropriate decisions to improve the situation in respect of narcological services, but 'had not been able to elicit their complete implementation by the leaders of the local organs'. Such failures of the Public Health Ministry were condemned by the inspectors as showing a lack of compassion for those suffering from alcoholism. The report also noted the high incidence of recidivism following compulsory treatment. In conclusion, most blame was laid at the door of the Chief Administration for the Organisation of Medical Help of the USSR Health Ministry, with the poor quality of its local health managers identified as a crucial weakness.

Treatments of a voluntary kind have become increasingly popular in the light of the relative failure of the state narcological services to cope adequately with the problems of alcoholism. The methods of Drs Dovzhenko and Shichko have already been noted. In the Shichko method, the patient's compulsion is held to be the result of a 'psychological programme', and so the answer is for him to be 'deprogrammed' of that compulsion in a series of psychotherapeutic sessions.[49] The Dovzhenko method is also based on psychotherapy, and has to do with 'mediated psychotherapy',[50] whereby the doctor actively influences the patient with the aim of putting him into a state of stress. The subject's brain is then 'encoded', so as to ensure an intolerance of alcohol.

Although both these methods have the enthusiastic support of the Sobriety Society, they are viewed with suspicion by orthodox medicine; the Shichko method was even banned for a time.[51] Nonetheless, these forms of treatment have at least made their way into self-financing institutions and co-operatives, despite the occasional claims of quackery.[52]

THE RESULTS OF THE ANTI-ALCOHOL DRIVE

In the period from the publication of the May 1985 anti-alcoholism decree of the Central Committee of the CPSU, to the beginning of the year 1989, per capita alcohol consumption fell to approximately 3.6 litres (see Table 5.1). While, for instance, the amount of alcohol consumed in Tadzhikistan, Uzbekistan, Kirgiziya and Moldavia decreased by almost 3 times, consumption in the Baltic and Belorussian republics remained discouragingly high at between 4.6 and 6.2 litres per head of population.[53]

By 1988, the production of wines, spirits and beers had decreased by a half compared with 1984 levels. However, in comparison with 1987 there was an overall increase in the volume of production of 16 per cent; the output of dry and dessert wines went up by more than 33 per cent, cognac by 23 per cent, and vodka and other spirits by 16 per cent. The sale of alcoholic beverages increased by 11 per cent over the previous year; average consumption over the country rose by 10 per cent as compared with 1987.[54]

In an effort to regulate properly the retailing of alcohol, and in order to avoid such negative phenomena as the unruly queues which followed from the restrictions in opening times and the burgeoning of illicit distilling, the government deliberately increased the volumes of alcoholic beverages produced and sold (see also Table 5.1).[55] The reduction in the sale of alcoholic beverages following the implementation of the 1985 decree also left between 49 and 51 billion roubles of extra disposable income in the hands of the population. Unfortunately, the requisite additional consumer goods and services were not forthcoming to absorb such sums.

More hopefully, the 'drive' has had a positive effect on the indicators of the use of worktime and in overall labour discipline. Thus, in the first half of 1988, losses in worktime in industry and construction due to absenteeism, idling and unauthorised absences from the workplace decreased by 5 million man-days in comparison with 1985.

Table 5.1 Selected statistics on alcohol production and consumption

(A) Production of alcoholic beverages						
	1980	*1985*	*1986*	*1987*	*1988*	*1989*
Vodka/spirits (m. decals.)	295	238	147	123	142	182
Wines (grape) (m. decals.)	323	265	141	147	179	193
Champagne (m. bottles)	178	248	195	225	258	256
Cognac (m. decals.)	9.4	7.0	6.7	9.5	11.8	13.6
Beer (m. decals.)	613	657	489	507	558	602

Source: *Narodnoe khozyaistvo SSSR v 1989 g.* (Moscow: Finansy i statistika, 1990) p. 497.

(B) Disposal of total family incomes by blue and white collar workers (%) of family budget)					
	1975	*1980*	*1985*	*1987*	*1988*
Alcoholic beverages	3.6	3.6	3.0	2.6	2.8

(C) Disposal of total family incomes by collective farm workers (% of family budget)					
	1975	*1980*	*1985*	*1987*	*1988*
Alcoholic beverages	5.1	4.9	4.2	3.3	3.5

Source: *Sotsial'noe razvitie SSSR* (Moscow: Goskomstat SSSR, 1990) p. 115.

Table 5.1   continued

(D)   Sales of alcoholic beverages through state and co-operative trade
      sectors, including public catering (millions of decalitres)

	1975	1980	1985	1986	1987	1988
Vodka/spirits	261.9	293.9	251.2	156.6	123.6	136.9
Wines (grape)	313.9	347.8	307.2	172.9	156.4	184.7
Wines (fruit/berry)	136.1	137.3	79.6	16.6	0.3	n.a*
Cognac	6.9	9.2	8.5	8.8	9.4	11.3
Champagne	10.8	14.9	21.9	20.7	20.6	21.8
Beer	574.2	620.7	667.8	496.9	514.6	564.8

* Production ceased in 1988.

Source: *Sotsial 'noe razvitie SSSR*, p. 134.

Even with all of the above improvements, alcoholism and alcohol abuse are all the more widespread, and treatment costs run at about 1 billion roubles annually. In 1984 there were some 153 narcological clinics in operation throughout the country, whereas by 1988 the number had increased to more than 500.[56] As observed above, the narcological services are not yet geared up to coping with the problem, and the necessary steps have not been taken to develop the network of self-accounting narcological out-patient departments and anonymous treatment consulting rooms. The overall number of patients suffering from chronic alcoholism and alcohol psychosis, according to treatment-prevention institutions, is approximately 4.6 million, or 1.6 per cent of the population (the figure for the USA is 4.4 per cent). However, conventional wisdom sees the real Soviet figure as possibly 12 to 14 million, because of the tendency of abusers to avoid registration with narcological clinics. The incidence of alcohol-related illness has nonetheless decreased by 29 per cent since 1985, and alcohol-related deaths have fallen by about 50 per cent (see Tables 5.2 and 5.3).

Despite the gratifying reduction of 14 per cent in the number of alcohol-related road traffic accidents in 1986 as compared with 1985, by 1988 the figure had once more reached the 1985 level. The overall number of breaches of the anti-alcohol legislation remains stubbornly unchanged at about 10 million per year. For example, the number of people committing crimes while under the influence increased from 371 000 in 1987 to 379 000 in 1988, an increase of 2 per cent, and between 20 and 25 thousand of these involved under-age drinkers.[57]

Table 5.2   Causes of death: numbers and causes in 1986

	Total pop.		Urban pop.		Rural pop.	
	male	*female*	*male*	*female*	*male*	*female*
From psychiatric disorders	3 434	2 257	2 194	1384	1483	873
Of the latter, from alcohol and toxicomania	2 265	572	1 458	330	807	242
From cirrhosis of the liver	17 710	13 696	10 044	6914	7666	6782
Of the latter, from alcohol cirrhosis of the liver	814	310	492	165	322	146

Source: *Naselenie SSSR 1987* (Moscow: Finansy i statistika, 1988), p. 362.

Table 5.3   Incidence of alcohol-related illnesses among the population (per 100 000 pop.)

	1980	1985	1986	1987	1988	1989
Number of those diagnosed for the first time as suffering from alcoholism and alcohol psychosis	206	217	196	181	154	149
Number of those registered with medical institutions and diagnosed as suffering from alcoholism and alcohol psychosis	1235	1613	1618	1628	1598	1494

Note: In 1988 it was calculated by treatment-prevention institutions that there were 9.8 million people suffering from mental illness, including 4.6 million suffering from alcoholism, as against 4.5 million of the latter in 1985.

Source: *Narodnoe khozyaistvo SSSR v 1989 g.* (Moscow: Finansy i statistika, 1990) p. 225.

Surveys of the ways in which people apportion their leisure time show that young men up to the age of 25 years working in industry spent on average one and half hours per week on physical culture and sports, and women of the same age group spent a mere 20 minutes per week in such pursuits. Only around 20 per cent of workers ever engaged in physical culture or sports, one of the chief reasons being the lack of sports equipment, which was on average one third below the norm. Public demand for sports clothes, facilities, and equipment went systematically unsatisfied.

In relating the intentions of the anti-alcohol drive to the actual results achieved, it must be concluded that it has been a failure. Despite occasional positive outcomes, alcohol-related crime remains high, and there has been a worrying increase in the amount of under-age drinking. Indeed, in September 1988 N. I. Ryzhkov, Chairman of the USSR Council of Ministers reported on the problem of overcoming the negative tendencies attendant upon the retailing of alcoholic beverages, such as the loss of time and scandalous disorders among people queuing for alcohol.[58] Ryzhkov remarked that in the course of the previous three years queues at retail outlets had grown by a half, because of the sharp reduction in the sale of alcoholic beverages consequent upon reduced output and a contraction in the number of retail outlets (by 55 per cent over the country as a whole during that period).

In addition, such factors as the failure to increase the production of consumer goods, the sharp increase in the amount of sugar being sold (by 18 per cent between 1985 and 1987) and other substances traditionally used for the manufacture of illicit alcohol, led to the passing of a resolution of the Politburo on 12 October 1988, 'On the Course of the Implementation of the Decrees of the Central Committee of the CPSU on Problems of Intensifying the Struggle Against Drunkenness and Alcoholism'. It was noted that 'the wide possibilities which had been created for intensifying the struggle against drunkenness and alcoholism have not been used as they should have in many regions, and have not been reinforced by scrupulous daily observance'. The resolution went on to point out that the failure to solve one of the most complex of social problems was due in considerable measure to the reliance upon 'administrative measures and the organising of noisy, short-lived campaigns'.[59] In addition, the party organs had failed to enrol the combined forces of society in the struggle.

Despite concluding with a formulaic insistence upon the continuation of the struggle based upon the guidelines laid down in the 1985 decrees, the resolution effectively argued the main reasons for the failure of those decrees. Thus, rather than the New Jerusalem of an abstemious society confidently anticipated in the legislation and by its propagandists, the idea of the 'moderate drinking' culture has caught on, abetted by the state's concern at the loss to the exchequer of alcohol revenues. In addition, there would seem to have been a mature, if disillusioned, realisation that this experiment in social engineering, typically Soviet in its employment of decrees from above, had been completely misconceived; ironically, a revolutionary attempt at change had been made using the instruments of the command-administrative system, which could not hope to eradicate deeply-ingrained cultural patterns in short order and in isolation from an overall restructuring of Soviet society.

In the Soviet government's struggle against alcohol abuse, the principal gain seems to have been the realisation that the changing of social consciousness is neither quick nor simple. In the Soviet context this means, in effect, the need for a humanisation of attitudes to the drinker, democratisation of the treatment-rehabilitation process and of the sobriety movement as a whole, the introduction of new economic and social mechanisms in treatment-prevention work based on self-accounting and cooperation, and 'the stimulation in the people of a sense of self-preservation, so that they will consciously choose the sober and healthy way of life'.[60]

Notes

1. T. Korzhikhina, 'Bor'ba s alkogolizmom v 1920–1930–kh godakh', *Voprosy istorii*, 1985, no. 9, p. 21.
2. E. P. Lanovenko et al., *P'yanstvo i prestupnost': Istoriya, problemy* (Kiev: Naukova dumka, 1989).
3. Korzhikhina, 'Bor'ba', p. 21.
4. Ibid.
5. Ibid., p. 23.
6. Ibid., p. 24.
7. Ibid., p. 26.
8. L. D. Miroshninchenko, 'Istoriya bor'by s p'yanstvom i alkogolizmom v 20–30–kh godakh', *Voprosy narkologii*, 1990, no. 3, p. 57.
9. Ibid., p. 58.
10. V. G. Treml, 'A Noble Experiment? Gorbachev's Anti-Drinking Campaign', in M. Freidburg and H. Isham (eds) *Soviet Society Under Gorbachev: Current Trends and Prospects* (Armonk, NY: Sharpe, 1987).
11. *Vedomosti Verkhovnogo Soveta SSSR*, no. 21 (22 May 1985), item 370.
12. *Pravda*, 16 June 1985, p. 1.
13. *Sovetskaya Rossiya*, 19 September 1985, p. 1.
14. *Pravda*, 29 May 1985, p. 1.

15. *Trezvost' i kul'tura*, 1989, no. 6, p. 5.
16. Ibid., no. 10, p. 1.
17. Ibid., no. 10, p. 2.
18. Ibid., no. 12, p. 24.
19. Ibid., no. 12, p. 25.
20. Ibid., no. 3, p. 24.
21. Ibid., no. 3, p. 25.
22. Ibid., no. 3, p. 25.
23. Ibid., no. 3, p. 26.
24. Ibid., no. 3, p. 28.
25. Ibid., no. 7, p. 5.
26. Ibid., no. 12, p. 24.
27. Ibid., no. 12, p. 24.
28. Ibid., no. 12, p. 25.
29. Interviews with staff of VNTsIIS for Narcology of the USSR Ministry of Health, Moscow, December 1989.
30. *Trezvost' i kul'tura*, 1988, no. 1, p. 23.
31. Ibid., 1989 no. 5, p. 13.
32. Ibid., no. 5, p. 14.
33. Ibid., 1988, no. 1, p. 24.
34. Ibid., no. 1, p. 25.
35. Ibid., no. 1, p. 24.
36. *Sotsialisticheskaya zakonnost'*, 1989, no. 11, p. 54.
37. Interview data (see note 29).
38. *Trezvost' i kul'tura*, 1989, no. 5, p. 14.
39. Ibid., 1988, no. 12, p. 40.
40. Ibid., no. 12, p. 41.
41. Ibid., no. 6, p. 40.
42. *Meditsinskaya gazeta*, 26 March 1989, p. 4.
43. Ibid.
44. Ibid.
45. Ibid.
46. Ibid.
47. *Trezvost' i kul'tura*, 1987, no. 10, p. 15.
48. *Meditsinskaya gazeta*, 1 February 1989, p. 3.
49. *Trezvost' i kul'tura*, 1989, no. 10, p. 15.
50. Ibid., no. 12, p. 2.
51. Ibid., no. 10, p. 2.
52. Ibid., no. 12, p. 3.
53. *Vestnik statistiki*, 1989, no. 6, p. 54.
54. Ibid., p. 55.
55. Ibid., p. 56.
56. Ibid., p. 61.
57. Ibid.
58. 'O nekotorykh negativnykh yavleniyakh v bor'be s p'yanstvom i alkogo-lizmom', *Izvestiya TsK KPSS*, 1989, no. 1, pp. 48–51.
59. Ibid.
60. *Trezvost' i kul'tura*, 1990, no. 8, p. 3.

6 Sex Differentials in Mortality in the Soviet Union

W. Ward Kingkade and Eduardo E. Arriaga

In almost every country of the world today women live longer than men. In all likelihood, the differential is produced by the interplay of biological parameters together with social conditions. Typically, the absolute difference between male and female life expectancies at birth is relatively small at high mortality levels, but becomes greater once mortality has fallen. The reduction in mortality from infectious and parasitic diseases has lowered female death rates relative to those of males at every age, suggesting an innate advantage of women that asserts itself once exogenous factors (which may include adverse social norms and practices) are counteracted. In most developed countries the excess of female over male life expectancy at birth is about six to seven years; the difference is somewhat narrower in developing countries which have achieved low mortality (for example, Cuba, Costa Rica and China).[1] Certain industrialised countries, most notably in Eastern Europe, exhibit a trend of progressively increasing excess male mortality in adulthood. The increases are largely attributable to causes of death presumed to respond to lifestyle patterns such as smoking and alcohol consumption, including cancer and cardiovascular conditions as well as accidents and poisonings. This paper examines one of the most extreme examples of such excess of male mortality: the Soviet Union.

The historical evolution of the sex differential in Soviet mortality appears unremarkable up to rather recent times. Over most of the twentieth century Soviet mortality declined due to control of infectious diseases, resulting in the familiar pattern of greater increases in female as compared to male life expectancy at birth (see Table 6.1). However, beginning in the mid-1960s reported life expectancies of both sexes began to fall, with greater declines among males than females. As a result, the sex differential in life expectancy at birth

Table 6.1   Official life expectancies at birth in the Soviet Union from 1896 to 1989

| Period | Life expectancy at birth | | |
	Male	Female	Difference
1896–1897	31.3	33.4	2.1
1926–1927	41.9	46.8	4.9
1938–1939	44.0	49.7	5.7
1955–1956	63.0	69.0	6.0
1958–1959	64.4	71.7	7.3
1960–1961	65.3	72.7	7.4
1962–1963	65.4	72.8	7.4
1964–1965	66.1	73.8	7.7
1966–1967	65.7	73.8	8.1
1968–1969	64.9	73.7	8.8
1970–1971	64.5	73.5	9.0
1972–1973	64.4	73.4	9.0
1974–1975	63.7	73.1	9.4
1976–1977	62.9	72.6	9.7
1978–1979	62.5	72.6	10.1
1980–1981	62.3	72.5	10.2
1982–1983	62.8	73.0	10.2
1984–1985	62.9	72.7	9.8
1985–1986	64.2	73.3	9.1
1986–1987	65.0	73.8	8.8
1987	65.1	73.8	8.7
1988	64.8	73.6	8.8
1989	64.6	74.0	9.4

Note: The 1896–1897 and 1926–1927 figures refer to the European territories of the Russian Empire and the Soviet Union, respectively.

Sources: Based on Demograf1cheskii ezhegodnik SSSR (Moscow: Finansy i statistika, 1990), p. 390, and A. G. Vishnevsky and A. G. Volkov, Vosproizvodstvo naseleniya SSSR (Moscow: Finansy i statistika, 1983), pp. 297–99.

continued to grow, reaching the level of about 9 years by 1970 and rising above 10 years by 1980. Soviet accounts attribute the unfavourable mortality trends and the resultant sex differential in life expectancy at birth to increases in adult mortality from accidents and degenerative diseases associated with a complex of lifestyle factors including alcoholism, smoking and unhealthy diets. Gorbachev's anti-alcoholism campaign and a programme to expand the coverage of diagnostic checkups represent attempts to respond to this situation. Perhaps partly as a result, life expectancy for both male and female populations of the USSR has risen since 1985. Although the recent improvements have narrowed the sex differential in Soviet life expectancy at birth, its current level of 8.8 years remains one of the largest in the world.

The purpose of this paper is to decompose the unusually large sex differential in Soviet mortality in terms of the contributions of specific causes of death. The paper is organised in the following manner. First, the mortality differential at each age is analysed by causes of death. Second, the contributions of each age group to the difference in life expectancy at birth are examined. Third, the major groups of causes of death and the most significant single causes of death contributing to the differential are investigated. Finally, the contribution of the causes of death to the life expectancy differential is analysed within those age groups where the mortality differential is the largest. Thereafter the results are discussed in relation to Soviet accounts of lifestyle factors affecting mortality and public health programmes.

MORTALITY DIFFERENTIALS BY AGE

The sex differentials in mortality can be analysed from an absolute or relative point of view. From an absolute point of view, the sex differential in mortality observed among infants declines rapidly by age until age 15. From age 15 the differential increases; at age 45 it becomes larger than among infants, and continues increasing with age. At ages 65 to 74, 3 per cent of the females die, while 6 per cent of the males do (Figure 6.1-A, and Table 6.2).

In relative terms, the pattern is completely different: it is in young adult ages where the differentials are the largest. At ages 25 to 34, male mortality is 3.5 times higher than female mortality, although the absolute difference is rather small (Figure 6.1-B, and Table 6.2).

CONTRIBUTION OF CAUSES OF DEATH TO THE DIFFERENTIAL IN MORTALITY

The main causes of death responsible for the sex differential in mortality are not the same in all age groups. Main causes of death vary over age essentially in terms of three broad age groups: infants, young adults and older adults (including the elderly).

The reader should keep in mind that this report discusses only

Figure 6.1–A   Age specific mortality rates by sex, Soviet Union, 1985

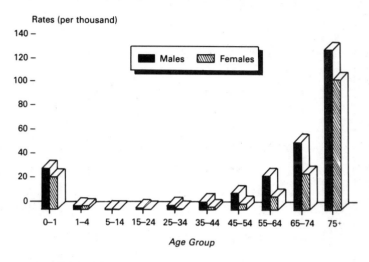

Source: See Table 6.2.

Figure 6.1–B   Absolute and relative sex differential in mortality by age, Soviet Union, 1985

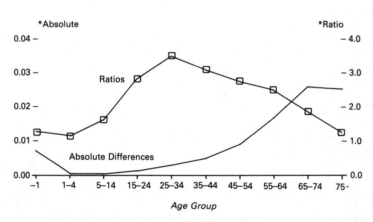

* Absolute differential refers to the difference of male and female central death rates in each age group. Relative differential is the ratio of male to female central death rates in each age group.

Source: See Table 6.2.

Table 6.2 Mortality rates by sex, age groups and groups of causes of death, Soviet Union, 1985

Age group and sex	All causes	†A	B	C	D	E	F	G	H	I	J	K
−1 *M	33.79	5.07	.11	.10	11.41	1.14	.41	3.65	9.27	1.29	.45	.90
F	26.87	4.38	.10	.10	9.38	.98	.32	3.12	6.29	1.05	.70	.44
1–4 M	2.81	.43	.09	.01	1.16	.56	.04	.13	.00	.20	.04	.14
F	2.50	.40	.08	.02	1.09	.43	.04	.12	.00	.17	.04	.11
5–14 M	.67	.02	.07	.01	.05	.30	.01	.03	.00	.08	.02	.07
F	.42	.02	.05	.02	.05	.14	.01	.03	.00	.07	.01	.02
15–24 M	1.79	.04	.09	.08	.05	.71	.03	.02	.00	.12	.48	.18
F	.63	.04	.07	.05	.04	.15	.02	.02	.00	.12	.09	.03
25–34 M	3.70	.12	.18	.37	.09	1.31	.11	.01	.00	.18	.98	.34
F	1.06	.05	.19	.13	.05	.19	.04	.01	.00	.17	.16	.05
35–44 M	6.93	.29	.71	1.55	.30	1.76	.33	.02	.00	.32	1.18	.48
F	2.26	.06	.61	.45	.09	.34	.12	.01	.00	.24	.24	.10
45–54 M	13.87	.41	2.81	4.55	.92	2.04	.70	.02	.00	.51	1.34	.58
F	5.08	.07	1.51	1.71	.23	.50	.27	.01	.00	.32	.30	.14
55–64 M	28.04	.55	7.46	12.01	2.48	1.83	1.27	.01	.00	.74	1.13	.56
F	11.27	.09	3.07	5.56	.58	.52	.53	.01	.00	.49	.27	.15
65–74 M	55.94	.53	11.59	32.64	5.55	1.32	1.82	.01	.00	1.23	.84	.41
F	30.12	.12	5.06	20.66	1.77	.53	.88	.01	.00	.64	.30	.15
75+ M	134.14	.52	12.41	99.54	13.76	1.68	2.32	.01	.00	2.31	1.22	.36
F	108.94	.18	6.25	91.74	6.59	1.08	1.50	.01	.00	.82	.51	.26

† Groups of causes of deaths:
Group A: Infectious and parasitic
Group B: Malignant neoplasms
Group C: Circulatory system
Group D: Respiratory system
Group E: All accidents except group K
Group F: Digestive system
Group G: Congenital malformations
Group H: Perinatal and early infancy
Group I: Other classified causes
Group J: Other causes unclassified
Group K: Accidents caused by machinery and cutting and piercing instruments.

* M and F represent male and female respectively.

Source: Calculated from a Soviet life table (Ward Kingkade, 'Recent Trends in Adult Soviet Mortality', paper presented at the Population Association of America, Chicago, 1987), and deaths information by cause and age (Ministerstvo zdravookhraneniya SSSR, 'Statisticheskie materialy', *Sovetskoe zdravookhranenie*, no. 1, 1988, pp. 66–74).

differentials in mortality, and that the levels of mortality are not discussed. For instance, the Soviet Union still has high levels of mortality from diseases of the respiratory system and infectious and parasitic diseases among infants compared to the levels observed in Western societies. Infant death rates from these two groups of causes represent half of the total infant mortality rate. However, the largest sex differential in Soviet mortality among infants is due not to these diseases but to mortality from causes classified under the category of conditions of the perinatal period and early infancy.

Infant mortality. Almost half of the sex differential in infant mortality is due to causes classified as congenital malformations, perinatal mortality and diseases of early infancy. Between one third and one fourth of the differential is due to diseases of the respiratory system, and around one tenth to infectious and parasitic diseases (See Figure 6.2-A and Table 6.2).

Mortality at ages 25 to 34. The sex differential in mortality in this age group seems similar to those in most Western countries: male accidents are the greatest contributor to the mortality differential. Nonetheless, diseases classified under the category of 'other' almost contribute as much as accidents (Figure 6.2-B and Table 6.2). This group of 'other' contains a residual of classified causes of death with small mortality sex differentials, and such causes of death which have not been classified as homicides, suicides, and violence. The excess male mortality from 'unclassified' causes is unusually high in the Soviet Union.

Mortality at ages 35 to 44. The mortality pattern of this age group resembles the previous age group. Male accidents are the largest contributor, while diseases of the circulatory system contribute approximately one fourth of the differential. As in the previous age group, a large proportion of the differential is due to 'other causes' (Figure 6.2-C and Table 6.2).

Mortality at Ages 45 to 54. From age 45 and above, diseases of the circulatory system are always the largest contributors to the sex differential in mortality. In this particular age group, the contribution to the sex differential made by accidents is lower than in the preceding age groups, while cancers and diseases of the respiratory system begin to make significant contributions (Figure 6.2-D and Table 6.2).

Figure 6.2   Sex differentials in mortality by selected age groups and main causes of death, Soviet Union, 1985

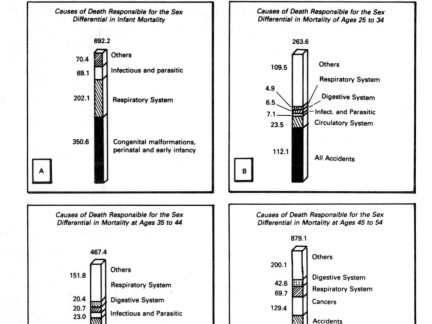

Note: Each bar represents the difference in mortality rates between sexes in the indicated age group.

Figures: per hundred thousand.

Source: See Table 6.2

However one should not be misled by this. Even in this age group, the absolute contribution to the differential by accidents is larger than the absolute contribution at ages 25 to 34.

Mortality at Ages 55 to 64.   Slightly over three fourths of the sex differential in mortality in these ages is due to the 'expected' causes of death: cardiovascular conditions, cancers, and diseases of the respiratory system. While the relative contribution to the sex differential in

Figure 6.2 (continued)

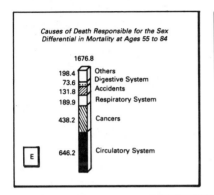

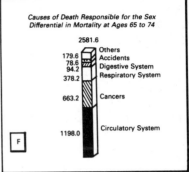

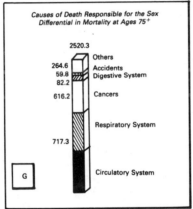

Note: Each bar represents the difference in mortality rates between the sexes in the indicated age group.

mortality by accidents is reduced, the differential due to diseases of the respiratory system starts to become more significant (Figure 6.2-E and Table 6.2).

Mortality Differentials at Ages 65 to 74. The trend observed in the previous age group continues in this one. The sex differential in mortality is completely dominated by three groups of diseases: those of the circulatory system, cancers, and those of the respiratory system, with the latter increasing its relative contribution (Figure 6.2-F and Table 6.2).

Mortality Differentials at Ages 75 and over.   The distinctive aspect of the differentials at these ages is that the absolute and relative contributions of the diseases of the respiratory system have significantly increased, and have become the second most important contributor – almost the same as the contribution made by the diseases of the circulatory system (Figure 6.2-G and Table 6.2).

CONTRIBUTION OF THE SEX DIFFERENTIAL IN MORTALITY TO LIFE EXPECTANCY AT BIRTH

The mortality differentials described above have definite effects on life expectancy at birth. Hence, the overall sex differential in life expectancy at birth can be decomposed into the contributions of sex differentials in mortality within specific age and cause of death categories.[2]

Decomposition of the Sex Differential in Life Expectancy at Birth by Age and Cause of Death

The sex differential in mortality during the first year of life produces a differential of almost half a year in life expectancy at birth (Figure 6.3 and Table 6.3). From age 1 to 15 years, the contributions are rather small. Thereafter they start to increase rapidly, achieving a maximum at the age group 55 to 64 years. The sex differential in mortality in this ten-year age group is responsible for an astonishing contribution of two years of life to the differential in life expectancy at birth. 80 per cent of the total difference of life expectancy at birth between the sexes (8 years) is produced by the mortality sex differential at ages 25 to 75.

Contribution to the Sex Differential in Expectancy at Birth by the Sex Differential in Mortality in Each Cause of Death

As in most developed countries, the sex differential in mortality over all ages from diseases of the circulatory system produces the largest differential in life expectancy at birth between males and females. In the case of the Soviet Union, these diseases produce a differential of more than two and a half years of life (Figure 6.4 and Table 6.3). The second largest contribution to the sex differential in mortality is made by the group of causes pertaining to all kinds of accidents, followed by malignant neoplasms. The fourth largest contribution is made by a residual group of causes which includes causes with practically no sex

Figure 6.3   Contribution to the sex differential in life expectancy at birth by the sex differential in mortality at each age group

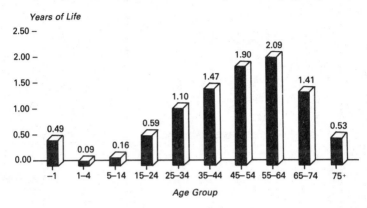

Note: Each bar represents the number of years of life contributed to the sex differential in life expectancy at birth by the sex differential in mortality in each age group.

Source: See Table 6.3.

differential in mortality, deaths pertaining to ill-defined causes, and three causes which were classified together with the ill-defined group: homicides, suicides and violence. Finally, the fifth largest contribution was produced by the group of diseases of the respiratory system. The sex differentials in mortality in these five groups of causes of death produce an astonishing sex differential in life expectancy at birth of 8.5 years. This difference of years of life generated by such diseases is one of the largest in the world.

Diseases of the Circulatory System.   The sex differential in mortality from ischemic diseases contributes almost two years of life to the sex differential in life expectancy at birth. This contribution is slightly smaller than the one produced by the sex differential in accident mortality (Figure 6.5 and Table 6.4). Approximately one quarter of the difference is due to infarcts; and the rest, 1.5 years, to 'other' ischemic diseases for which there is no detailed information. Cerebrovascular diseases add about half a year of life to the sex differential in life expectancy at birth.

Accidents.   One of the distinctive aspects of the sex differential in life expectancy at birth in the Soviet Union in relation to western

124

Table 6.3 Contributions of years of life to the sex differential in life expectancy at birth by each group of causes of death and age groups, Soviet Union, 1985

Age group	All causes	†A	B	C	D	E	F	G	H	I	J	K
								Groups of causes of death				
−1	.49	.05	.00	.00	.14	.01	.01	.04	.21	.02	−.02	.03
1–4	.09	.01	.00	.00	.02	.04	.00	.00	.00	.01	.00	.01
5–14	.16	.00	.01	.00	.00	.10	.00	.00	.00	.01	.01	.03
15–24	.59	.00	.01	.01	.01	.29	.01	.00	.00	.00	.20	.07
25–34	1.10	.03	−.01	.10	.02	.47	.03	.00	.00	.00	.34	.12
35–44	1.47	.07	.03	.35	.06	.45	.07	.00	.00	.03	.30	.12
45–54	1.90	.07	.28	.61	.15	.33	.09	.00	.00	.04	.22	.09
55–64	2.09	.06	.55	.80	.24	.16	.09	.00	.00	.03	.11	.05
65–74	1.41	.02	.36	.65	.21	.04	.05	.00	.00	.03	.03	.01
75+	.53	.01	.13	.16	.15	.01	.02	.00	.00	.03	.01	.00
Total	9.83	.32	1.37	2.69	1.00	1.90	.36	.05	.21	.19	1.20	.54

† Groups of causes of deaths:

Group A: Infectious and parasitic
Group B: Malignant neoplasms
Group C: Circulatory system
Group D: Respiratory system
Group E: All accidents except group K
Group F: Digestive system

Group G: Congenital malformations
Group H: Perinatal and early infancy
Group I: Other classified causes
Group J: Other causes unclassified
Group K: Accidents caused by machinery and cutting and piercing instruments.

Source: as Table 6.2

Figure 6.4   Contribution to the sex differential in life expectancy at birth by the sex differential in mortality for each cause of death

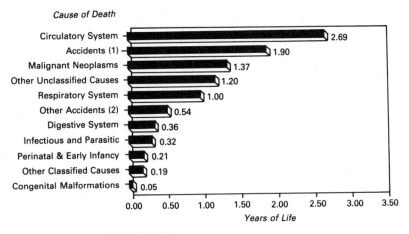

(1) Except Group K, Table 6.3
(2) See Table 6.3, Group K

Note: Each bar represents the number of years of life contributed to the sex differential in life expectancy at birth by the sex differential in mortality for each cause of death over all ages.

Source: See Table 6.3.

European countries is that traffic accidents make a relatively small contribution to the sex differential in life expectancy at birth: less than one third of a year (Figure 6.6 and Table 6.4). In the case of the Soviet Union, the group of unclassified accidents is the largest contributor. This group includes 'other accidents' as well as deaths from late effects of accidents and injuries from machinery and cutting instruments. The detailed accident categories producing a significant contribution to the sex differential in life expectancy at birth are poisonings and drownings, both together sharing four fifths of a year.

It seems that traffic accidents at young adult ages in the Soviet Union do not have as great an impact on the sex differentials in life expectancy at birth as is the case in Western societies. The contribution of young adult ages to the sex differential in life expectancy at birth is the result of a mixture of causes of deaths.[3]

Cancer.   Among all cancers, those of the respiratory system are the ones producing the largest sex differential in life expectancy at birth.

Figure 6.5   Contribution to the sex differential in life expectancy at birth by the sex differential in mortality from diseases of the circulatory system

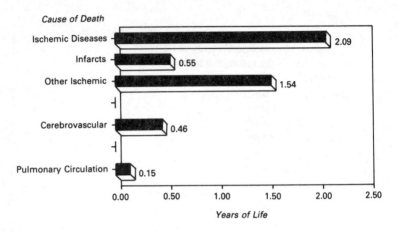

Note: Each bar represents the number of years contributed to the sex differential in life expectancy at birth by the sex differential in mortality for the given cause of death.

Source: See Table 6.4.

The excess of male over female mortality from cancers of the trachea, lung and bronchus makes the life of males three quarters of a year shorter than that of females (Figure 6.7 and Table 6.4).

Respiratory System.   Unfortunately, only half of the year contributed by diseases of the respiratory system to the sex differential in life expectancy at birth can be explained by specific causes (bronchitis, asthma and pneumonia). The rest of the diseases of the respiratory system are aggregated together as 'other respiratory' (Figure 6.8 and Table 6.4).

Contribution of the Sex Mortality Differential by Age and Cause of Death to the Differential in Life Expectancy at Birth
The analysis of the contribution of mortality differentials by age and cause of death to sex differentials in life expectancy shows certain features that could be of interest for policy making. In ages 45 to 75, diseases of the circulatory system are the dominant contributors to the reduction of male longevity relative to that of females. From age

Table 6.4 Contributions of years of life to the sex differential in life expectancy at birth by selected causes of death and age groups, Soviet Union, 1985

Age group	All causes							†Causes of death						
		1	2	3	4	5	6	7	8	9	10	11	12	13
–1	.11	.00	.00	.00	.00	.00	.00	.00	.00	.00	.00	.00	.00	.00
1–4	.04	.00	.00	.00	.00	.00	.00	.00	.00	.00	.00	.00	.00	.00
5–14	.07	.00	.00	.00	.00	.00	.00	.00	.00	.00	.00	.00	.00	.00
15–24	.22	.00	.00	.00	.00	.00	.00	.00	.00	.00	–.01	.00	.00	.01
25–34	.47	.03	.01	.00	.02	.00	.00	.01	.04	–.01	–.02	.00	.00	.02
35–44	.84	.07	.02	.02	.08	.00	.00	.03	.18	–.05	–.03	.01	.00	.02
45–54	1.37	.07	.03	.03	.12	.00	.01	.04	.31	–.07	–.04	.02	.01	.02
55–64	1.74	.05	.01	.02	.08	.01	.01	.02	.17	–.05	–.03	.04	.01	.01
65–74	1.26	.02	.00	.01	.03	.00	.01	.01	.05	–.02	–.03	.04	.01	.00
75+	.47	.01	.00	.01	.03	.00	.01	.01	.05	–.01	–.01	.04	.00	.00
Total	6.58	.26	.08	.08	.34	.02	.02	.09	.76	–.21	–.15	.11	.03	.08

Age Group					†Causes of death								
	14	15	16	17	18	19	20	21	22	23	24	25	26
–1	.00	.00	.00	.00	.00	.11	.00	.00	.00	.00	.00	.00	.00
1–4	.00	.00	.00	.00	.00	.01	.00	.00	.00	.01	.01	.00	.00
5–14	.00	.00	.00	.00	.00	.00	.00	.00	.00	.00	.04	.02	.01
15–24	.00	.00	.01	.00	.00	.00	.00	.00	.00	.02	.06	.10	.01
25–34	.01	.05	.02	.01	.00	.01	.00	.01	.01	.11	.08	.11	.03
35–44	.07	.19	.04	.04	.01	.03	.01	.03	.03	.15	.05	.07	.03

continued on page 128

Table 6.4 continued

Age group	All causes	†Causes of death												
		1	2	3	4	5	6	7	8	9	10	11	12	13
45–54	.12	.35	.04	.08	.01	.04	.04	.07	.05	.13	.03	.04	.03	
55–64	.14	.44	.03	.17	.03	.03	.09	.12	.05	.06	.01	.02	.01	
65–74	.07	.36	.02	.17	.03	.01	.09	.10	.03	.01	.00	.01	.01	
75+	.03	.15	.00	−.02	.00	.01	.07	.07	.01	.00	.00	.00	.00	
Total	.44	1.54	.15	.46	.08	.26	.30	.40	.18	.48	.29	.37	.13	

† Causes of death:

Cause 1: Bacterial
Cause 2: Cancer of lips, mouth, throat
Cause 3: Cancer of esophagus
Cause 4: Cancer of stomach
Cause 5: Cancer of colon
Cause 6: Cancer of rectum
Cause 7: Cancer of larynx
Cause 8: Cancer of trachea, lungs, bronchi
Cause 9: Cancer of breast
Cause 10: Cancer of cervix, uteral
Cause 11: Cancer and hyperplasia of prostate
Cause 12: Leukemia
Cause 13: Ulcers

Cause 14: Infarcts
Cause 15: Other ischemia
Cause 16: Pulmonary circulation
Cause 17: Cerebrovascular
Cause 18: Arteriosclerosis, embolisms and thrombosis
Cause 19: Pneumonia
Cause 20: Bronchitis, asthma
Cause 21: Other breathing
Cause 22: Cirrhosis and other liver
Cause 23: Poisonings
Cause 24: Roadway accidents
Cause 25: Drowning
Cause 26: Falls and fires

Source: as Table 6.2.

Figure 6.6   Contribution to the sex differential in life expectancy at birth by the sex differential in mortality from accidents

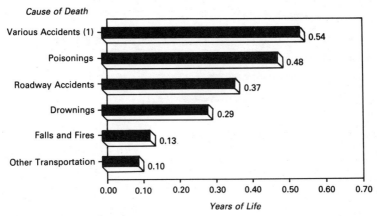

(1) See Table 6.3. Group K.

Note: Each bar represents the number of years contributed to the sex differential in the life expectancy at birth by the sex differential in mortality for the given cause of death.

Source: See Table 6.4.

Figure 6.7   Contribution to the sex differential in life expectancy at birth by the sex differentials in mortality from cancers

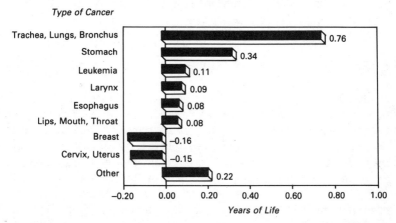

Note: Each bar represents the number of years of life contributed to the sex differential in life expectancy at birth by the sex differential in mortality in each cause of death over all ages.

Source: See Table 6.4.

Figure 6.8   Contribution to the sex differential in life expectancy at birth by the sex differential in mortality in selected causes of death

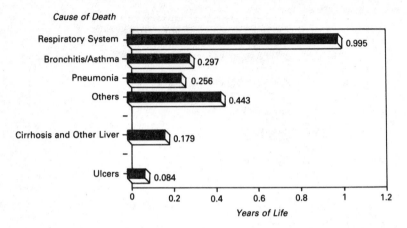

Note: Each bar represents the number of years of life contributed to the sex differential in life expectancy at birth by the sex differential in mortality in each cause of death over all ages.

Source: See Table 6.4.

15 to age 44, accidents are the main suppressors of male life expectancy. Cancers are also significant at ages 45 to 74 years (Figure 6.9 and Table 6.3).

EXPLANATIONS: LIFESTYLES

In the Soviet public health literature, social factors and lifestyles occupy a prominent position in explanations of the sex differential in mortality. Two sets of lifestyle factors are typically considered: negative habits, and the stresses of modern living. Negative habits receive most attention, with special emphasis on alcoholism. Consumption of alcoholic beverages, a common element of celebrations in the traditions of the Russian nationality, became during the post-war era a customary activity on paydays, holidays, and social gatherings, undoubtedly facilitated by the massive production of liquor and limited availability of many alternative consumer goods in the postwar USSR.[4] About two thirds of the Soviet population are regular drinkers, while 6 per cent are classified as alcohol abusers.[5] Evidence from

Figure 6.9   Contribution to the sex differential in life expectancy at birth by the sex differential in mortality in indicated age group and cause of death

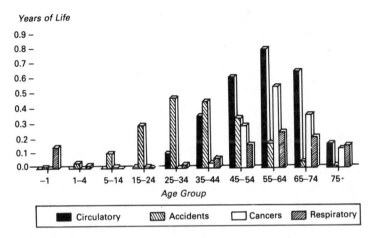

Note: Each bar represents the number of years of life contributed to the sex differential in life expectancy at birth by the sex differential in mortality in each cause and age group.

Source: See Table 6.4.

various urban areas in European Russia indicates that most adult women as well as men are drinkers.[6] However, males comprise the overwhelming majority of clinical alcoholics.[7] Alcohol consumption figures as a leading explanation in Soviet discussions of sex differentials in accident mortality and mortality from cardiovascular conditions.[8]

Second to alcoholism on the Soviet list of negative lifestyle elements is smoking. A majority of adult men and a growing proportion of women in the Soviet Union are smokers.[9] The majority of males become smokers prior to their nineteenth birthday.[10] Efforts to discourage smoking are handicapped, among other things, by the fact that a majority of doctors become smokers in medical school.[11]

Although Soviet women tend to fare better in terms of healthiness than do men on most lifestyle dimensions, this is not always the case: obesity is a notable exception. Recently published data for Moscow[12] indicate that adult women are overweight significantly more often than men, while other data indicate no appreciable difference between the sexes.[13] This may, at least in part, reflect the appetite-suppressing effects of smoking and heavy drinking among males, who might in the absence of these habits experience the adverse consequences of the cholesterol-laden Soviet diet more severely.

East European demographers have coined the term 'civilization diseases' to denote those causes of death which, paradoxically, become more widespread as people gain control over the physical environment.[14] Soviet authors regard the complexity and artificial rhythms of modern life as sources of stress which act to heighten mortality from degenerative disease.[15] A leading Soviet medical demographer[16] has advanced the argument that men tend to be employed in more rigorous mental or physical activities than women as a partial explanation for the greater longevity of women. While this position can be attacked on the grounds that women experience additional burdens related to childcare and housekeeping responsibilities,[17] there is also some evidence that Soviet women compensate by working less intensely.[18]

Another health-related behaviour with clear implications for sex differentials in mortality pertains to utilisation of health care itself. Soviet women in the young adult ages resemble their Western counterparts in being more prone than men to report themselves ill, taking more sick leave and making greater use of health service institutions than do Soviet males.[19] This may indicate that women take a more active approach to health maintenance than do men in these ages, which may contribute to the ultimate differential in mortality.

DISCUSSION

Although the available information on causes of death does not permit a fully comprehensive explanation as to why the Soviet Union has such a large sex differential in life expectancy at birth, the above analysis is suggestive of several factors which may underlie the observed Soviet differential. Starting with the young adult ages, deaths from poisoning provide one of the largest contributions to the sex differential in life expectancy at birth. The difference in mortality from poisonings is probably due to self-inflicted acts as well as involuntarily inflicted poisonings.[20] Some of the involuntarily inflicted poisonings could be intoxications resulting from working conditions; alternatively, they may be related to alcohol intoxication.[21] Obviously, an intoxicated person will be more prone to accidents than a sober individual, other things being equal. Moreover, alcoholism may lead to increased mortality in other disease categories by aggravating various chronic degenerative conditions, including cardiovascular disease as well as cirrhosis of the liver. In the Soviet literature alcoholism is even cited as a factor exacerbating the prevalence of infectious diseases such as tuberculosis.[22]

The sex differential in mortality from diseases of the circulatory system is not a surprise. In all societies for which data are available mortality from these causes is substantially higher among males as compared to females. However, the information on cardiovascular mortality should be analysed together with the data for mortality from certain cancers. Soviet males exhibit much higher mortality from cancers of the respiratory system organs than do Soviet females. This fact, together with the higher male mortality from diseases of the circulatory system, may be the result of a difference in smoking habits between Soviet men and women. Although national-level indices of smoking frequency and duration are not publicised in official Soviet statistical handbooks, a body of information is available from health studies conducted in various locations in the USSR. The evidence indicates that the majority of males begin to smoke before the age of 20, while among women smoking commences on average at a later age and in lower proportions.

Since working conditions for men and women probably resemble each other more in the Soviet Union than in Western societies, it does not seem probable that the larger sex mortality differential in the Soviet Union in comparison to Western societies would be from poisonings related to occupational sources. In all likelihood, the sex differential in mortality from poisonings is due to alcohol or substance abuse. On the other hand, mortality from cancer and diseases of the circulatory system is, at least partially, a consequence of habits, behaviour and factors that have accumulated during a long period of time. Because of the much higher male than female mortality from cancer in organs of the respiratory system and ischemic diseases, it is likely that smoking is responsible for shortening life among males more than females.

In the cases of poisonings and cancers as well as diseases of the circulatory system, male mortality may be reduced in certain ages by changing habits. The change of habits can be induced by special educational programmes. If such programmes are carried out in the Soviet Union and people change their damaging habits, male mortality may be reduced during the next decade and the differential in life expectancies between males and females will become smaller.

AFTERWORD

Another recent initiative in Soviet public health is a programme to expand the coverage of preventive medical examinations, with the ambitious goal of bringing all members of the Soviet population under regular, repeated clinical observation (*dispanserizatsiya*).[23] This approach represents an appropriate strategy for dealing with degenerative diseases, whose symptoms tend to become acute only at a point where the disease has progressed too far to remedy many of its effects. However, at present less than half the former Soviet population is covered by medical exams. Complete coverage is articulated as a long-term goal to be approached gradually over the remainder of this century. Additional measures in the area of health services are contained in the guidelines for restructuring the health system adopted in November 1987. These include sorely needed increases in expenditures on medical facilities and supplies, which had declined as a share of the Soviet state budget during the 1970s. The legislation also relaxes many of the restrictions on the autonomy of medical personnel and institutions.

Notes

1. US Bureau of the Census, *World Population Profile: 1987* (Washington DC, 1987) Table 10.
2. The technique used was presented in Edward Arriaga, 'Measuring and explaining the change of life expectancies', *Demography*, vol. 21, no. 1 (February 1984) pp. 82–96; and 'Changing trends of mortality decline during the last decade', a paper presented to the seminar on Biological and Social Correlates of Mortality, Tokyo, November 1984.
3. See Alain Blum and Alain Monnier, 'Recent mortality trends in the USSR: new evidence', *Population Studies*, vol. 43 (1989), pp. 211–41.
4. V. L. Abushenko, 'Sovershenstvovanie kul'tury obraza zhizni kak uslovie preodoleniya p'yanstva i alkogolizma', in Sektor sotsial'nykh problem alkogolizma i narkomanii Instituta sotsiologii SSSR, *Za zdorovyi obraz zhizni. (Bor'ba s sotsial'nymi boleznyami). Materialy nauchnoi konferentsii*, 3 vols (Brest, 1988) vol. 2, pp. 80–1. See also G. G. Zaigraev, 'Alkogol'naya situatsiya: ob"ekt profilakticheskogo vozdeistviya', *Sotsiologicheskie issledovaniya*, 1985, no. 4, pp. 47–54, and Zaigraev, 'O nekotorykh osobennostyakh profilaktiki p'yanstva', ibid., 1984, no. 4, pp. 96–105.
5. M. A. Kamaliev and T. A. Siburina, 'Teoreticheskie i organizatsionnye problemy pervichnoi profilaktiki osnovnykh khronicheskikh neinfektsionnykh zabolevanii v SSSR i za rubezhom', in Ministerstvo zdravokhraneniya SSSR, Vsesoyuznyi nauchno-issledovatel'skii institut

mediko-tekhnicheskoi informatsii, *Meditsina i zdravokhrananie. Seriya sotsial'naya gigiena, organizatsiya i upravlenie zdravokhraniem: Obzornaya informatsiya*, 1988, vyp. 2, p. 21.

6. Zaigraev, 'Alkogol'naya situatsiya'.
7. T. N. Grosheva and S. N. Bokov, 'Nekotorye sotsial'nogigienicheskie aspekty zhenskogo p'yanstva i alkogolizma v usloviyakh krupnogo goroda', *Zdravokhranenie Rossiiskoi federatsii*, 1986, no. 6, pp. 27–30.
8. See for instance N. Ya. Kopyt, 'Mediko-sotsial'nye faktory preodoleniya p'yanstva i alkogolizma', ibid., 1985, no. 12, pp. 3–7; I. V. Polyakov *et al.*, 'Nekotorye osobennosti smertnosti naseleniya krupnogo goroda', ibid., 1984, no. 4, pp. 16–19; T. V. Ryabushkin and R. A. Galetskaya, *Naselenie i sotsialisticheskoe obshchestvo* (Moscow: Finansy i statistika, 1983); and M. S. Bedny, *Mediko-demograficheskoe izuchenie narodonaseleniya* (Moscow: Statistika, 1979).
9. I. Lavrova and E. Kuido, 'Kurenie i ego posledstviya dlya zhizni cheloveka', in D. I. Valentei (ed.), *Nashe zvorod'ye* (Moscow: Finansy i statistika, 1983); A. N. Baikina, 'Sem'ya i sotsial'nye bolezni molodezhi', in *Za zdorovyi obraz zhizni*, vol. 3, pp. 53–4.
10. O. S. Radbil' and Yu. M. Komarov, *Kurenie* (Moscow: Meditsina, 1988) pp. 17–18.
11. Kamaliev and Siburina, 'Teoreticheskie', p. 47.
12. L. V. Chazova *et al.*, 'Integral'nyi podkhod k profilaktike osnovnykh khronicheskikh neinfektsionnykh zabolevanii', *Sovetskoe zdravokhranenie*, 1989, no. 1, pp. 3–7.
13. Kamaliev and Siburina, 'Teoreticheskie', p. 22.
14. N. A. Tolokontsev, 'Zdorov'e cheloveka i abiologicheskie tendentsii v sovremennykh usloviyakh i obraze zhizni', in I. I. Smirnov, ed., *Obshchestvennye nauki i zdravokhranenie* (Moscow: Nauka, 1987).
15. A. G. Vishnevsky and A. G. Volkov, *Vosproizvodstvo naseleniya SSSR* (Moscow: Finansy i statistika, 1983); L. P. Shakhot'ko, *Vosproizvodstvo naseleniya Belorusskoi SSR* (Minsk: Nauka i tekhnika, 1985), p. 83; Tolokontsev, 'Zdorov'e cheloveka'.
16. Bedny, *Mediko-demograficheskoe izuchenie*.
17. N. Rimashevskaya, 'Aktual'nye problemy polozheniya zhenshchiny', *Sotsialisticheskii trud*, 1987, no. 7, pp. 50–8.
18. T. V. Ryabushkin, *Trudovye rezursy i zdorov'e naseleniya* (Moscow: Nauka, 1986).
19. Rimashevskaya, 'Aktual'nye problemy'; Ryabushkin, *Trudovye rezursy*; A. Ya. Yurkevich, 'Kakie faktory vliyayut na zabolevaemost' rabochikh', in E. K. Vaslie'eva, ed., *Bud'te zdorovy* (Moscow: Finansy i statistika, 1982), pp. 40–52.
20. Ward Kingkade, 'Demographic trends in the Soviet Union', in John Hardt and Richrd Kaufman, eds., *Gorbachev's Economic Plans*, vol. 1 (Washington DC: Government Printing Office, 1987), pp. 166–86.
21. Kopyt, 'Mediko-sotsial'nye faktory'.
22. For example, see N. M. Rudoi and T. Ch. Chubakov, *Tuberkulez legkikh i alkogolizm* (Moscow: Meditsina, 1985).
23. G. A. Novgorodtsev, G. Z. Demchenkova and M. L. Polonsky, *Dispanserizatsiya naseleniya v SSSR* (Moscow: Meditsina, 1984).

7 Disabled 'Afgantsy': Fighters for a Better Deal
Jim Riordan

If there is one subject concerning the USSR that has evaded the attention of Western scholars it is the disabled.[1] Partly this is because few are equipped to study the crippled, insane, blind or deaf. In any case, even within the (former) USSR, the dimension of the disabled population and the extent and effectiveness of its treatment is little publicised; for decades virtually nothing on the subject reached the foreign eye. *Perestroika* is changing that. But it is the agitation by Afghan veterans for a better deal for themselves and other disadvantaged groups in the population, especially the handicapped, that has done much to bring publicity, and force action.

The return home of the 'Afgantsy', the 'lost generation' of 528 000 veterans of the Afghan war, some grotesquely scarred in body and mind and prematurely aged by their harrowing experience of war, has already caused considerable discomfort for the authorities all over the USSR. As Sergei Popov, producer of a documentary film about the war veterans (*Vozvrashchenie – The Return*) says, 'This is a war that is going to stay with us for a very long time. The psychological cost of Afghanistan will go on throughout our lifetime and will probably be passed on to our children too'.[2] Just as the French and US veterans affected the political and social state of their countries after the Algerian and Vietnamese wars respectively, so the 'Afgantsy' have been seriously affecting the social and political health of Soviet society.

SOVIET REPORTING OF THE WAR

At a time when bad news was no news, up to Gorbachev's accession to power in March 1985 the Soviet media were either silent on the goings-on in Afghanistan and their repercussions at home, or portrayed morale-boosting military triumphs, progressive Afghan social programmes and civilian casualties inflicted by bandits armed to the teeth by their imperialist masters. The writer Julian Semenov, for example, sent back reports from Afghanistan of the dollar bills and pornographic photos found on the bodies of dead guerillas, of mines camouflaged as children's toys, and the dedication of Soviet army doctors in treating civilian casualties.[3]

It was precisely the mind-numbing 'cowboys and Indians' approach, typical of the pre-Gorbachev era, which – like propaganda on unremitting economic successes at home about which the public knew differently – gave rise to profound scepticism and dissatisfaction with Afghan reporting. Allied to this were widespread rumours, the angry letters of relatives and eyewitness reports by returning soldiers; they all painted quite a different picture from the official one. So irritated was one soldier about the war reporting – 'you write one thing', he told a visiting journalist, 'and we see it entirely differently' – that he was determined to take up journalism on his return, 'to write about Afghanistan myself. They [Soviet papers] write such crap it makes you sick'.[4] Another fighting man expressed a wish to become a war historian 'to study this war and analyse it in depth'.[5]

The father of a sergeant killed in Afghanistan wrote to *Pravda* in early 1988 complaining of

> the very scanty, fragmentary and sometimes unrealistic coverage of events in Afghanistan by our mass media . . . Our press was evidently unprepared for our having to stay there for several years . . . The papers used to write about avenues of friendship that our soldiers were planting, about our doctors delivering Afghan women's babies and the Afghan Army routing the bandits.[6]

Such uncritical reporting continued even after Gorbachev came to power, but a new realism was making itself felt, especially in the *glasnost'* 'flagships' like *Moscow News*, *Sobesednik* and *Ogonek*, and in local papers like *Avrora*, *Moskovskii komsomolets*, *Leningradskii rabochii* and *Molod Ukrainy*. When, for example, the Leningrad writer Leonid Bogachuk reported back in early 1988 from his Komsomol-sponsored tour, he wrote that

> we can no longer depict the situation in Afghanistan in black and white terms as if the *dushmany* are all bad and against us, while the Afghan government and army are all good and for us. It's all far

more complex . . . Our papers often portray . . . [the *dushmany*] only as savage, bearded villains. The fact is that they vary. I've often had occasion to make friends with them.[7]

Not all writers grasped the nettle of the war. Some deliberately remained silent, refusing to play the piper's tune either in novels about the war or in reports from battle zones. This may have been their form of silent protest, but it did not pass unnoticed: the author Kim Selikhov, writing in *Literaturnaya gazeta*, complained that 'not many writers are concerned with the exploits of Soviet soldiers in Afghanistan . . . The internationalist fighting men are hoping that their favourite writers will visit them, people like Yevtushenko, Voznesensky, Aitmatov, Gamzatov, Okudzhava and Rasputin'.[8]

In a series on the war in early 1988 in *Ogonek*, Artem Borovik wrote in the style of the soldier's raw realism, slang and political cynicism, with few holds barred: of death and amputation, of cowards and heroes, of a young Soviet girl blown to pieces on her wedding day,[9] and of torture – like Soviet soldiers having incisions made around their waists and their skin pulled up over their heads like an undershirt.[10] The former sports star and now war correspondent Alexander Vasilevsky, writing in the Leningrad Komsomol literary monthly *Avrora*, described the sad cases of soldiers initially fighting well, getting wounded, receiving honours, being hospitalised, then breaking down, of 'others who get themselves soft jobs in the canteens and yet others who avoid frontline action yet beat their breasts on going home, calling themselves valiant "Afgantsy"'.[11]

Glasnost' also affected feature and documentary films. The semi-documentary film 'It isn't easy to be young' has a hero declaring 'War is war . . . Wounded, cripples, dead of whom we never hear. Somewhere in a long article you very occasionally read a couple of terse lines. All the rest is to the tune of triumphal marches . . . It's painful and hurtful'.[12] Bitter criticism of Moscow's TV war coverage gradually found its way from the front into the press, especially of the false make-believe war for the cameras:

When they shot war scenes, they'd often have the reporter sitting on an armoured tank, hoarsely breathing into the mike: 'Listen to the shooting . . .' as tired soldiers just back from a raid fired into the air in imitation of heavy fighting. But that isn't war! We used to call such TV scenes 'for show only' and dreamed of one day someone telling the truth about our tough jobs.[13]

Such TV scenes and lyrical newspaper reports of 'Soviet soldiers entertaining Afghans with songs and dances and mending their tractors'[14] were clearly much despised and resented by many fighting men. A stark article by Laura Tsagolova in the popular youth weekly *Sobesednik* in January 1988 exposed the horrors of the war as no other reporting had done: of soldiers 'counting the days to demob, hating the heat and dust', of 'death and starvation', of 'recurring nightmares, drug addicts and nerve-shattered veterans', of the lasting damage that war had inflicted on soldiers and of the realities, not the romance, of war. As one man put it, 'I wouldn't wish such an experience on anyone. War is death. War takes the lives of utterly innocent people as well as butchers and foes. Where's the romance in that?'[15] The article gained overwhelming approval for its telling of the harsh truth. As a member of the Writers' Union put it,

I fully share the author's discontent with the long, to put it mildly, delicate portrayal of the war by the media. What were we trying to hide and from whom? From the public? The public knew. From mothers? Mothers were tending the graves of their sons in village graveyards. Thank God, the time of concealing the truth is past.[16]

Mothers, in fact, did not remain silent as they tended graves. A letter from a mother of two conscripts, published in the Ukrainian Komsomol paper *Molod Ukrainy*, outspokenly criticised the war, questioned official explanations for the Soviet presence, and condemned the eulogistic nature of media coverage.[17] If the official reporting of the war provoked anger and disbelief, especially among the 'Afgantsy' themselves, the callous official treatment of, and bureaucratic indifference to, soldiers returning to 'a land fit for heroes' helped turn mumbles of discontent into roars of open resentment, even rebellion.

SOVIET WAR CASUALTIES

Official Soviet statistics on war casualties were released only after withdrawal had begun, and then subsequently revised in 1989. The latest figures are 13 833 dead, 35 478 wounded and 330 missing.[18] Altogether, some 150 000 men were deployed at the height of the war, with an average of 110 000 usually rotated on an annual basis.[19] War losses were therefore less than 3 per cent of total fighting men.

By contrast, the USA lost 56 146 men and committed 537 000 troops at the height of its war – approximately four times the Soviet figure – but sustaining just over 4 per cent dead of the fighting contingent.[20] Each nation's losses were, of course, but a fraction of other people's lives lost (1 313 000 in Vietnam's case,[21] and at least one million in Afghanistan's).

Some people have cast doubt on the official Soviet casualty statistics: 'What sort of battle activities could have produced such results for one side to suffer meagre losses? Perhaps our lads were engaged merely in planting trees and transporting goods, so that the 3 per cent is a consequence of road accidents and gardening misfortunes? The military ought to release the real figures on our losses in Afghanistan'.[22]

If the figures have been played down (although they do not differ substantially from US losses in Vietnam – under 3 per cent to just over 4 per cent) this would fit the pattern of official statistics on invalids generally: 'We have some 7m invalids – that is, less than 2.5 per cent of the population. These figures are seriously open to doubt. In France, where the standards of living and health care are higher than in the USSR, the invalid average in the mid-1970s was over 6 per cent of the population. That ours are two and a half times lower shows merely that many actual invalids are not recognised as such officially and receive no pension'.[23] The periodical *Argumenty i fakty* estimated the real figure in 1990 as between 28 and 30 million.[24]

In July 1990 a new magazine, *Sotsial'naya zashchita* (Social Protection), carried an interview in its first number with Anatoly Osadchikh, Head of the Social Labour Rehabilitation Unit of the State Labour Committee. He reported that 'we treat every year some 73 million chronically sick – that is, incurable cases. That's not forgetting alcoholics, drug addicts and the homeless who also include plenty of sick people. If even half of these people are invalids, we have a good 30 million (not the 7.5m officially recognised as being invalids). I can't give a more exact figure because we still have no precise understanding of what constitutes an invalid'.[25] It has to be added that official statistics do not include anyone under 16 years of age. The real figure of invalids, for cross-cultural comparison, would therefore seem to be in the region of 30 to 35 million, or over 10 per cent of the population.

MEDICAL PROBLEMS

By the nature of the war, many casualties resulted from mines that left several thousands of young people without arms, legs or sight. The war accordingly put an immense strain on an area of the Soviet medical service that is, by international standards, appallingly backward – that is, in the provision of artificial limbs, wheelchairs and equipment for the blind. The situation had actually worsened since 1960:

> Between 1921 and 1960 there were some 400 disabled workshops bringing in quite a profit, and 58 rest homes and sanatoria for the disabled. In 1960 the government decided that the invalid problem had been resolved and, as a result, all those workshops were transferred to the ministries for local and light industry, and the rest homes and sanatoria to the trade unions.[26]

All the same in 1990 there were 170 enterprises at which invalids were working.[27] Indeed, if able to work, all disabled are entitled to free job placement services. By law all enterprises are required to reserve places for disabled war veterans (though not for other groups), including those of Afghanistan. The major problem with job placement is the inability of the authorities actually to get disabled people to the workplace owing to the lack of accessibility of public transport and buildings to wheelchair-bound invalids. Another problem is the lack of special equipment that would enable invalids to perform suitable and useful (profit-making) job tasks.

The lack of educational opportunity, of mobility and technology, signify that a high percentage of the handicapped are unable to hold down a regular job. In addition, the low level of pensions means it is hard for those unable to work even to survive – without family support. As a result, a large number of handicapped people work in sheltered workshops and live in homes for the disabled. As an American expert comments,

> Because these homes for the disabled have poor government financial support, yet have production plans to fulfil, and because lack of mobility effectively confines many of the handicapped to these homes, the homes are only a step above the worst place for the handicapped in the Soviet Union – labour camps.[28]

Solzhenitsyn and others have reported the existence of large labour camps for the disabled as well as sizeable handicapped sectors of regular labour camps. The uncommonly high death rates reported for these camps may be put down to the imposition of a harsh camp regime on physically weak inmates.

As the veil is slowly being drawn aside from the plight of the Soviet handicapped, other areas are being exposed that lack proper information. For example, while it is known that Britain has 28 and West Germany 53 rehabilitation centres for the handicapped, 'no one knows how many the USSR has because we simply don't have anything called by that name. All we can say is that there are far fewer than are needed'.[29]

Few people who have lived in or visited the Soviet Union in the last few decades can have been unaffected by scenes of limbless World War II veterans pushing themselves along by stumps on makeshift wooden trollies on streets and subways, or begging outside churches or railway stations. The Soviet Union has virtually no special facilities for the disabled by way, for example, of lifts or ramps. As *Moscow News* has put it, 'Have you ever seen special lanes for invalid wheelchairs, or special lifts in cinemas or theatres? Have you ever heard about matinee performances for such people? We have doomed our disabled to a life confined to four walls'.[30]

Being confronted with the new widescale war misery, the authorities are being reminded of the shame of the 'welcome home' for soldiers in 1945. 'We simply thrust them as far out of sight as possible, along with their ramshackle, homemade carts. Have they ever forgiven us?'[31] Yet, today, more than forty years on, with no domestic wartime destruction to cope with, equipped with international medical experience and with a far stronger economy, the situation is little changed. The stream of complaints, the creation of a host of pressure groups and charities endeavouring to safeguard the rights of 'Afgantsy', all-too-frequent tales of degrading medical services and the snubbing by party and Komsomol officials, demonstrate the woeful state of affairs. On their return home the 'Afgantsy' frequently find that society does not recognise the debt they think it owes them for doing their 'internationalist-patriotic duty'. *Pravda* has reported receiving 'a torrent of letters . . . about official callousness and indifference towards the needs of the veterans'.[32] The paper later mentioned 'a pile of letters . . . [citing] more and more instances of indifference, callousness and unwillingness even to lift a finger to provide elementary assistance or simply humane attention or to intervene in the fates of young men who have endured the harsh school of Afghanistan'.[33]

It was only in the summer of 1987 that the first meeting of the newly-formed Paraplegic Sports Federation took place. A year later the first USSR Paraplegic Games were held and the first-ever Soviet disabled team – 13 blind athletes – took part in the Paralympics, which traditionally follow the summer Olympic Games (that year, 1988, held in Seoul, South Korea).[34] At the end of the year, 15 Soviet handicapped athletes, including four Afghan veterans, took part in the Disabled Skiers' Challenge competition in North America, organised by disabled Vietnam veterans. One Soviet participant, Lev Indolev, compared in *Moscow News* the treatment he received in the USA and the rudeness, ignorance and lack of concern he had met in the USSR. In the USA 'there was not a single instance when I felt discomfort or dependence on others'.[35]

Estonia (with 45 000 registered disabled out of a population of 1.5 million) was the first Soviet republic to draft a law (in 1988) on making all new buildings conform to standards that take account of the disabled.[36] Elsewhere, conditions for the handicapped are pitiful and, in recreational terms, often totally absent. Even the Soviet capital, Moscow, 'has no recreation equipment, coach, doctor or sports amenities for the handicapped'.[37]

But it is the lack of basic rehabilitation equipment that is causing most discontent, especially among the 6500 registered Afghan disabled. It is largely the 'Afgantsy' themselves and their supporters who have harried the authorities and brought shameful official negligence towards the disabled to public notice. They caused *Pravda* to admit that Soviet invalids 'are essentially people with no rights'.[38] One writer states that 'the very status of marginals is a reproach to society in that many of them can put their handicap down to the predatory use of their labour power, the dreadful state of medical and living facilities, and the psychologically unbearable conditions of their infernal existence caused by an unfeeling society'.[39] One example of exploitation of invalids was given by *Moscow News* in late 1989, revealing that at the Soviet 'Army Factory' the maximum monthly wage for invalids of 40 roubles (an invalid gets a rate of 60 kopecks for printing 1000 labels, for which the enterprise receives 3 roubles 90 kopecks) caused 300 of them to stage a strike and a protest march to Red Square.[40]

Under the circumstances of *glasnost'*, it is not so easy to conceal unseemly sights and unpalatable truths from the public. The writer

Bogachuk, for example, is engaged in collecting 'material about the hospital treatment of wounded 'Afgantsy', about their dilemma at home and the negligent attitudes towards the disabled'.[41] In early 1988 the popular daily *Sovetskaya Rossiya* detailed the cases of three severely disabled conscripts who had returned home 'to find their problems had only just begun'. It told of how one man who had lost both his legs was forced to live in squalid, overcrowded conditions, how another had to wait ages for the supporting straps for his artificial limbs, and how a third, partially sighted, was refused permission to live in the same hostel as his wife. As the paper concluded, 'The survivors of Afghanistan doubtless bear terrible scars in terms of their nerves and peace of mind. But they are not to blame. We are to blame for our hardhearted inability to care – a quality our people were once renowned for'.[42]

A special military hospital was opened in the early 1980s in the Crimean town of Saki, but despite the advanced medical treatment there, the disabled are sent out into the world with 'antediluvian crutches and artificial limbs, and a wheelchair shortage'.[43] A correspondent, visiting the hospital in December 1987, wrote of the 'bloody calluses caused by his [the ex-commander of a paratroop-assault platoon] artificial limbs . . . Both of his legs were amputated. His new limbs standing in the corner were a mockery of advanced technology or even humanitarian treatment'.[44]

An artificial limb specialist with over 30 years' experience, writing in *Ogonek*, reveals the heartlessness of the bureaucratic system as it has developed over the years:

> The situation is absurd: we never get to see the patients, we make the limbs on spec. The lab technician does the measuring, noting down a bend here, tuck there, add a bit on there. Then off to the workshop. No one cares whether it actually fits. Apart from the patient, of course. But nobody asks him. So a person gets an artificial limb and can't use it. Or he suffers, is rubbed raw, hobbles along gritting his teeth in pain, finally arriving for refitting at our workshop on the other side of town. . . . Artificial limbs are actually made for accounting, for meeting the plan; never for those who need them. . . . Our equipment is so outworn that Americans wouldn't believe their eyes if they were to see what we work with.[45]

It was partly to cut through the bureaucracy that the party Politburo transformed a number of clinics and sanatoria into treatment and rehabilitation centres for Afghan veterans; they include the Rus Sanatorium on the shores of the Ruz reservoir just outside Moscow, the Kasanai Sanatorium in the north of the Ferghana valley in the foothills of the Tien Shans, the Lesnaya Polyana Sanatorium in the Ukraine and the Baikal Sanatorium by Lake Baikal.[46] On the whole, however, the disabled generally come low on the list of social priorities. That they do have such low priority – by contrast, say, with sports stars on whose sophisticated equipment foreign currency is lavished, or the élite who can afford imported brandies and cigarettes – can only lie heavily on the consciences of Soviet leaders. The Afghan war began, after all, as long ago as 1979. As the head of the Saki army hospital, Captain Mikhail Babich, says with obvious envy and regret, 'I have often seen new models of artificial limbs in foreign medical journals and I always wonder why our lads get such inferior treatment'.[47]

At least the sanatorium and hospital patients can comfort one another in their misfortune. Once outside, they are often on their own and the problems multiply. 'Bribes have to be paid for artificial limbs, even poorly made ones'. 'The military authorities frequently provide an inferior 30 h.p. Zaporozhets invalid car rather than the prescribed 40 h.p. one'. 'It's hard to get a job and accommodation, and a disabled veteran's pension is hardly enough even for a few months.'[48] The second category invalid pension, which many disabled veterans qualify for, is a mere 38 roubles 36 kopecks per month (about a sixth of the average industrial worker's monthly pay).[49]

Small wonder that veterans' councils and defence committees have sprung up, like the Afgantsy Association formed in July 1990; one of its first tasks was to speed up preparations for the construction of a monument bearing the names of all who had died in Afghanistan.[50] An eight-page newspaper illustrated in colour, *Kontingent*, came out in August 1989 published by the Orenburg Council of Soldier Internationalists, with news on events, lost comrades, monuments, poems and meetings between Afghan and World War II veterans. A whole range of charities, like the Wounded Soldiers' Aid Fund, have come into existence; for the first time since the early 1920s, the clergy are being allowed, even encouraged, to play their part in obtaining and dispensing charity. Informal organisations like the Foundation for Social Inventions are inventing and demonstrating new sports equipment for the disabled. And an umbrella organisation known as the All-Union Association of Rehabilitation of the Handicapped was set up in mid-1990, embracing such bodies as the Soviet Charity and

Health Fund, the All-Russia Invalid Society, the All-Union Council of War and Labour Veterans and the All-Union Association of Scientific and Technological Co-operatives and Enterprises.

Since the inauguration of the new Soviet parliament, the USSR Congress of People's Deputies, in May 1989, the disabled also have their own deputies, like Ilya Zaslavsky, himself disabled, and several disabled Afghan veterans. As the co-operative movement got under-way a number of co-ops sprang up to help the disabled 'Afgantsy', making artificial limbs and wheelchairs and collecting funds for build-ing and fitting out rehabilitation centres. Even such ventures, how-ever, were not without ulterior motives: 'some co-operatives include disabled 'Afgantsy' on their staff in order to use their documents to hide illegal transactions and reduce taxation'.[51]

PSYCHOLOGICAL PROBLEMS OF WAR

If the scars of a war-ravaged body are hard to heal, those of the mind present an almost insoluble problem, identical to that posed by some returning Vietnam veterans in the 1970s and often expressed in similar sentiments. It is significant that the Soviet Union has turned to the USA, inviting teams of American experts in the rehabilitation of Vietnam War veterans. As one American expert, Diana Glasgow, put it, 'The Russians were particularly troubled about the social and psychological integration of returning war veterans. They want to know tons about post-traumatic stress syndrome'.[52] And when Soviet and American veterans themselves have met, the scenes have often been moving: 'I've seen Soviet and American veterans embracing and sobbing on each other's shoulders. Only they know why they're shedding tears. They know what war is'.[53]

As one war-shocked Soviet veteran has put it, 'It's impossible to get used to the still of the night, to realise that someone running towards you isn't going to shoot you full of bullets, to know a mine won't explode beneath your feet'.[54] Then there are the recurring nightmares about lost comrades, the nocturnal screaming, like that of Igor Kulilenko: every night he wakes up in a sweat, screaming, calmed by his mother's words, 'Are you still fighting the war, my son?' As a *Sobesednik* journalist comments, 'Soldiers on returning home realise they can no longer live by the rules of war, yet they cannot adapt to their new life either. They find it hard and no one can help them'.[55]

As a writer in the Komsomol theoretical monthly *Molodoi kommunist* has put it, 'We don't know how to heal the wounds in the minds of the generation burned by war'. He lists recent newspaper reports:

The other day an 'Afganets' blew himself up with a grenade after traipsing from one office to another in vain.

The other day an 'Afganets' shot himself in the woods near Moscow.

The other day yet another 'Afganets' died of his wounds before help came.

Where on earth is our respect for and duty to those who came home?[56]

Some have turned to drink or drugs, as a number of reports indicate. Whether as many as over half Soviet military personnel in Afghanistan tried drugs, as US personnel had in 1971, may never be known.[57] All that Soviet sources have revealed are individual instances of drug taking, the testimony of mass drug taking by former fighting men, and drug trading with the 'mujahideen'.[58] A doctor refers to such people as having a

shattered mind as well as a shattered body . . . They need more than just hospital care. Without proper attention, support and friendly concern, they will never be able to lead normal lives. Only the people around them can give them such things. But, alas, such people often remain blind and deaf; worse still, some push the lads into seeking oblivion in drugs or drink.[59]

War memories evidently induce some to seek the oblivion of the vodka bottle or the heroin syringe. As one correspondent admitted on visiting a drug unit containing three 'Afgantsy', 'the boys are utterly alone, sick with a more serious affliction than drug addiction . . . They are suffering from memories that keep taking them back to the war'.[60] It is as yet unclear how many servicemen picked up the habit in Afghanistan, but instances have been cited of drugs being obtained from the rebels, many of whom fought on drugs.[61]

Yet other war-befuddled veterans have turned their back on society altogether. A letter to the youth weekly *Sobesednik* from 17 young men in Kaluga reports the forming of a veterans' commune which was engaged in building its own five-storey, 28-apartment block named 'Afgana', using 'our building skills to heal the wounds of war'.[62] There are also reports of some veterans turning to religion, though this has received little publicity. They seem to find the communal comfort and quiet contemplation of religion a boon.[63] Like the returning Vietnam veterans in the 1970s, some – perhaps the 'silent majority' – just wish to live quietly, trying to forget. Few, however, can pick up the pieces of their pre-Afghanistan lives and continue as before. Politically, it is the active vanguard or resistance movement that poses the greatest threat to the stability of society – whether for good or bad in terms of *perestroika* may well depend upon the pace and direction of that process.

THE 'AFGANTSY' RESISTANCE MOVEMENT

A consistent theme in media coverage of the 'Afgantsy' is the way that many refuse to accept with equanimity the slow pace of change and the Western youth culture that, to them, pervades society.

> They talk mostly about the life they've returned to and in which they can't live as they did before . . . They've come back with such purity in their hearts and clarity in their minds . . . These are the people the fatherland needs most today.[64]

The vivid contrast between military service and the materialistic, relatively 'easy' life at home, with its consumerist, hedonistic values, especially among young people untouched by war, is what seems to affect the conscripts most of all. A journalist writes of these 20-year olds that 'they have experienced the full horror of war . . . that has stamped itself upon them, changing something within them. They differ radically from their contemporaries'.[65] In a postscript on the film 'It isn't easy to be young', one of the participants admitted that initially he had turned to drink 'because I couldn't stand the sight of the speculators and wide-boys. They swagger about town like tin-pot gods. We've created them by our cult of materialism. The moment I see them I think of what our lads over there are suffering, the shells and mines, that terrible climate and homesickness. I feel more than intense hatred. I just don't know what has to happen for people to understand and feel how we feel'.[66]

One returning conscript, Alexander, says he seemed to have

'landed on another planet. Painted girls totter about, super-fashion-able guys meet each DJ's announcement of a tape by a group from "over there" [the West] with squeals of delight, and hiss our Soviet music'. Even four years after his return, he still 'looked at many things through different eyes. Something had changed within me'.[67]

Alexander tells the story of going to a comrade's wedding and seeing a waitress wearing a jumper with a stars and stripes badge with a 'Made in the USA' motif (reminding him of the same inscription on the mine that killed his best friend in Afghanistan); an uproar ensued and the police were called. His view of many youngsters was that

> They've forgotten the real value of life. I don't believe that if it came to it all those girls and boys in their fancy gear with foreign labels would defend their homeland. It was one such fellow who betrayed us in Afghanistan; we later discovered he had been a disco king back home.[68]

Because they find the authorities dragging their feet in tackling social ills, as well as what they regard as anti-Soviet behaviour on the part of young people, many 'Afgantsy' are setting up their own veterans' associations: the 'Green Hats' (after the hats worn by Soviet border guards), the 'Reservists', the 'Marines' and 'Internationalist-Soldier Councils', which all engage in what their members call 'military-patriotic education of young people'.[69] This sometimes involves meting out rough justice to those who do not share their patriotic ardour and perception of morality. A Reservist Council in Kirovsk, for example, is, according to its chairman Vladimir Klimov, an 'instrument of social justice' against 'yobs who waste their time on rock, empty chattering, senseless fighting and dishonest activities'.[70] Some critics have referred to them as 'punishment brigades' with misanthropic views, a pogrom mentality and Stalinist ideology, using anti-democratic methods to pursue their goals.[71]

It is here that the ex-conscripts sometimes overlap with the vigilante gangs like the *Lyubery*. (The *Lyubery*, who take their name from the Moscow industrial suburb of Lyubertsy, are self-appointed guardians of what they see as genuine Soviet values. Their 'patriotism' extends to trying to intimidate and cleanse society of all alien elements, primarily followers of Western fashion.) A vigilante gang called 'Waterfall' (*Kaskad*) in Kazan', whose long-term programme is 'to eliminate all groups harmful to society', confesses to having ex-conscripts as leaders and feels it necessary to act 'as in Afghanistan, inasmuch as there can be no success without military discipline'.[72] *Izvestiya* reports the neofascist *Pamyat'* Society making great efforts to recruit 'Afgantsy'.[73]

When a *Literaturnaya gazeta* journalist asked Vadim, ex-service-man and *Lyubery* member, whether 'the hatred [towards 'West-ernisers'] was being fomented by ex-conscripts', he was told, 'I shed blood, sweat and tears in Afghanistan . . . We did what needed doing. Never forget that'.[74] But the question went begging. Nonethe-less, it is admitted that the Ramboesque young thugs 'will follow the "Afgantsy" anywhere and show a great interest in martial arts camps.'[75] Perhaps the fury is understandable when the veterans find themselves taunted by youth gangs that call themselves the 'Penta-gon' and rename their districts 'California' and 'Washington'.[76]

Not a few adults would like to see the returning heroes given their head to try to instil some discipline and respect into dissolute youths. 'Outraged' of Adizhan (Uzbekistan) writes to the magazine *Smena*, warning that 'It is only a short step from fetishisation of imported rags to murder, from striving after an easy life to betraying the country'. The writer, a schoolmistress, feels that today's young people need the firm hand of the 'Afgantsy':

> War! Only merciless war on all these things. Instil maximalism in all moral issues. That same maximalism that the lads who call themselves 'Afgantsy' are now displaying, those who have had the whiff of gunpowder in their nostrils and have gone through hell in Afghanistan.[77]

What often irks the 'conquering heroes', however, is that society does not seem to appreciate the debt they feel it owes them for doing their duty. As one complains on his return home, 'There was no music, no bouquets, no speakers from the Komsomol'.[78] Officialdom seems wary of giving them responsibility to apply their zeal to civilian life. Lt Vladimir Kolinichenko, for example, complains that only two ex-conscripts had been made Komsomol secretaries in the whole of Moscow's 33 districts. 'They don't welcome people dedicated in deeds not words to the Soviet system.' Why? Because, it seems, '"the Afgantsy" stir things up, make people do work they're unaccustomed to'.[79] From Tadzhikistan comes a letter from Leonid Zhilnikov, chairman of an Internationalist-Soldier Club, writing that in the face of official hostility the Club had been forced to set up its own informal 'Komsomol detachment' – 'it's hard to exaggerate the aid from the

"Afgantsy",' he says, 'they'll go through hell for justice'.[80]

A young Latvian in the film 'It isn't easy to be young' says that the worst thing is 'not being taken seriously, being treated like little children, not being trusted . . . We want to change that, show what the "Afgantsy", dead and alive, have demonstrated . . . that their generation can and must be trusted'.[81] In the city of Kuibyshev, a 70-strong group of 'Afgantsy' even took over a district Komsomol committee for a month, calling itself the 'Opposition' (*Protivostoyanie*). Founded a few years before by veteran Valery Pavlov and engaging in 'boxing, wrestling and war games', they took over because of what they claimed was 'neglect of military-patriotic work in the district'; and they appointed Pavlov Komsomol chief. Surprisingly, the usurpers served out the month without official intervention.[82]

An even more challenging event took place in early November 1987 in Ashkhabad, capital of Turkmenia and near the Afghan frontier: some 2000 young men who had served in 'Afgana' staged a rally and camp, involving weapon handling, unarmed combat, target shooting and lectures, their aim being 'to define ways of improving the military-patriotic education of young people'.[83] The rally certainly had semi-official approval, though it clearly took the central authorities by surprise. As *Komsomol'skaya pravda* reported, 'Probably not everyone liked the idea of the rally being organised from below, on youth initiative'.[84] That the objective was not only to flush out 'bureaucrats' was apparent from the statement put out by one of the camp spokesmen:

> It was simpler in Afghanistan. We knew full well who the enemy was and who had to be destroyed. But you can't stick a bureaucrat up against a wall here, or scare a home-grown punk and drug addict with a machine gun. We have to find some other way.[85]

Not all those at the rally shared the disciplined approach of its leaders; reports mention veterans going on the rampage, 'staggering about drunkenly in their green army fatigues, trying to stop buses'.[86] Small wonder that some people are cautious about handing over responsibility to such 'muscular socialists'. As Vladimir Chernyshev, ten years in the paratroops and two years in Afghanistan, admits, 'There are some Soviet as well as Western voices that call us thugs (*golovorezy*)'.[87]

It later emerged that the rally had been the culmination of a spontaneous movement begun in 1985, as 'clubs and councils appeared like mushrooms after the rain'. Despite official opposition and unwillingness to help with provision of drill halls, uniforms and combat sports equipment, the 'Young Paratrooper' movement succeeded in co-ordinating activities and providing all that the state civilian agencies (but not the army, evidently) had refused. All the same, the problems of the 'Afgantsy' are plainly daunting, as a journalist covering the rally testifies:

> Committee work and drill are unending, at home they have to endure the wife's hysterics because she never sees her husband, at work their workmates murmur about them wanting this, that and the other, at college they are forever at odds with the authorities.

So why do they do it? 'Not for ourselves, but for those we left behind'.[88] A facile answer, but one that provides emotional fuel for their effort. They now have their own record distribution system, arranging to post records and tapes by such groups as the 'Blue Berets' and 'Waterfall' all over the country.[89]

This tentacled solidarity movement of resistance to what is vaguely perceived as unpatriotic, bureaucratic and effete values and actions is patently growing in size and significance. Where exactly it is heading its own members are no doubt uncertain; for the moment the 'Afgantsy' seem to possess no long-term coherent plans for political power, let alone for the overthrow of the current reforming leadership of the country. All that could alter if aspirations, aroused by Gorbachev's policies, find no satisfaction through their participation in shaping their own and the nation's destiny, and in receiving the attention and treatment they feel are their due. There are already right-wing groups, like *Pamyat'*, bidding for their allegiance should they seek an active opposition.

CONCLUSIONS

What is so unpredictable about the impact on Soviet politics and society of the 'Afgantsy', including those with the most genuine grumbles – the disabled – is that they are acting on a new stage, partly erected by the war, which is providing fresh, unprecedented opportunities for debate, co-ordinated action and opposition. In the USA, it was incomparably simpler for returning soldiers of various dispositions to find their niche, interest group, community, channel or medium for expressing protest, letting off steam or 'turning off' altogether. As the many studies show, however, few could completely escape from their war memories or discover a panacea for curing their mental wounds. In the former USSR today, society is in flux from the old totalitarian model to a more decentralised, open system that is increasingly providing scope for a range of interests by way of informal youth associations, independent clubs, co-operatives, charities, local and national elected councils, even extremist gangs and groups that may well facilitate the reintegration process or, at least, offer the 'Afgantsy' a 'safety valve' for letting off steam.

In the post-war period much of the progress in handicapped rights in economically-advanced Western nations has come from three factors. First, there have been the legal measures transferring the costs of handicapped participation in society to a wide variety of economic entities: to owners of buildings, managers of public transport and business people to prevent job discrimination. Second, there has been a proliferation of voluntary organisations, charities and pressure groups that have put pressure on government and businesses to safeguard the rights of the disabled, and that have themselves provided community services and mutual help facilities. Third, the revolution in rights for the handicapped has been accompanied by a revolution in technology – electronically-controlled wheelchairs, computers, speech synthesisers – which has produced equipment often developed by small venture capital companies.

In the Soviet Union, bureaucracy, economic backwardness and the monolithic state have all combined to hamper a similar development of the rights of the handicapped. Added to that are the deeply rooted attitudes of the Soviet people towards the handicapped; changing them will not be easy. As Peter Maggs has put it,

The intolerance of the Christian tradition for full participation by handicapped people in the life of society combines with the Potemkin village mentality of Soviet bureaucrats to create an atmosphere in which handicapped people can be kept out of the way. Many think that Stalin had wounded veterans shipped out of Moscow after the end of World War II, as an urban beautification measure.[90]

What the disabled ex-soldiers from Afghanistan have demonstrated already is that they are not prepared to put up with the 'feudal' conditions that their brothers returning from World War II tolerated in circumstances of Stalinist repression. They want the best that money can buy, the relatively active life enjoyed by American and West European invalids. And if they do not get it, woe betide the leader or party that tells them their place is at the back of the queue.

Notes

1. The first Western book meriting attention on the Soviet disabled came out in 1989: see W. O. McCagg and Lewis Siegelbaum (eds), *The Disabled in the Soviet Union* (Pittsburgh: University of Pittsburgh Press, 1989).
2. V. Matizen, 'Ot otchayaniya k nedezhde', *Isskustvo kino*, 1987, no. 4, p. 37.
3. See *Tribune de Genève*, 18 November 1985, and Martin Walker, *The Waking Giant* (London: Michael Joseph, 1986) p. 136.
4. Artem Borovik, 'Desant severnee Kabula', *Ogonek*, January 1988, no. 4, p. 12.
5. Victor Turshatov, 'How those returning from Afghanistan are faring in wheelchairs', *Moscow News*, 13 December 1987, p. 13.
6. P. Studenikin, 'Ya vas v Afganistan ne posylal . . .', *Pravda*, 5 August 1987, p. 3.
7. Leonid Bogachuk, 'Pishu ob Afganistane . . .', *Leningradskii rabochii*, January 1988, p. 4.
8. Kim Selikov, 'Po trudnoi dorozhke', *Literaturnaya gazeta*, 14 October 1987, p. 14.
9. Borovik, 'Desant', pp. 9–12.
10. See Bill Keller, 'Russia's divisive war. Home from Afganistan', *The New York Times Magazine*, 14 February 1988, p. 28.
11. Alexander Vasilevsky, 'Moi zemlyaki v Afganistane', *Avrora*, 1988, no. 2, p. 35.
12. Juris Podniecs, Abram Kletskin, Yevgeny Margolin, 'Nashi soavtory', *Avrora*, 1987, no. 9, p. 20.
13. Laura Tsagolova, 'Snova snitsya voina', *Sobesednik*, January 1988, no. 3, p. 11.
14. Ibid.
15. Ibid.
16. Sergei Yesin, 'Nazyvaya imena', *Sobesednik*, March 1988, no. 12, p. 3.
17. *Molod Ukrainy*, 7 December 1986, p. 3.
18. See 'The heavy toll of Afghanistan', in *Soviet Weekly*, 16 September 1989, p. 14.
19. Martin Walker, 'Afghan war toll topped 13 000', *Guardian*, 26 May 1988, p. 9; 'They're home', *Moscow News*, June 1988, p. 2.
20. See Guenter Lewy, *America in Vietnam* (New York: Oxford University Press, 1978) p. 451. In Algeria, France also committed half a million men (in 1958). See Charles Gallagher, *The United States and North Africa* (Cambridge, MA: Harvard University Press, 1963) p. 275.

21. Lewy, *America*, p. 451.
22. See V. Gavrilyan, 'Dolzhny znat' pravdu', *Sobesednik*, no. 46, November 1989, p. 7.
23. *Na izlomakh sotsial'noi struktury* (Moscow, 1987) p. 238.
24. A. Deryugin, 'Ne khotim milostyni', *Argumenty i fakty*, no. 14, 7–14 April 1990, p. 8.
25. A. I. Osadchikh, 'Invalid: o nem i dlya nego', *Sotsial'naya zashchita*, no. 1, July 1990, p. 48.
26. Deryugin, 'Ne khotim'.
27. Osadchikh, 'Invalid', p. 50.
28. Peter Maggs, 'Legal rights of the handicapped in the USSR', paper given to the Fourth World Congress for Soviet and East European Studies, Harrogate 1990, p. 8.
29. Osadchikh, 'Invalid', p. 49.
30. I. Bobrova, 'Standing on your own two feet', *Moscow News*, 6 March 1988, no. 10, p. 2.
31. Victor Turshatov, 'How those who are returning from Afghanistan are faring in wheelchairs', *Moscow News*, 13 December 1987, p. 13.
32. A. Simurov, P. Studenikin, 'Net blagodarnosti v ikh serdtsakh', *Pravda*, 25 November 1987, p. 6.
33. Studenikhin, 'Ya vas v Afganistan ne posylal . . .'
34. Witnessed by the author.
35. Lev Indolev, 'No place like home?', *Moscow News*, no. 2, 1990, p. 16.
36. Bobrova, 'Standing on your own two feet'.
37. V. Ponomareva, 'Yeshche odna pobeda', *Sobesednik*, September 1987, no. 37, p. 12.
38. *Pravda*, 26 August 1988, p. 8.
39. A. G. Vishnevsky (ed.), *Perestroika v chelovecheskom izmerenii* (Moscow: Progress, 1989) p. 196.
40. Ivan Vilkin, 'Driven to extremes', *Moscow News*, no. 41, 1989, p. 14.
41. Leonid Bogachuk, 'Pishu ob Afganistane . . .'.
42. Quoted in Christopher Walker, 'Ordeal in Afghanistan haunts Soviet soldiers', *The Times*, 16 January 1986, p. 3.
43. Turshatov, 'How those returning . . .'.
44. Ibid.
45. Valery Baidanov, 'Pomogite vstat' na nogi . . .', *Ogonek*, no. 21, May 1989, pp. 22–4.
46. Colonel I. Dynin, 'Ostaemsya v stroyu . . .', in *Pul's: voyenno-politichesky almanakh*, vypusk 1 (Moscow: Voennoe izdatel'stvo, 1989) p. 173.
47. Turshatov, 'How those returning . . .'.
48. Ibid.
49. See *Sobesednik*, 1988, no. 16, pp. 12–13.
50. See *Moscow News*, no. 11, 1990, p. 2.
51. Dynin, 'Ostaemsya', p. 173.
52. Michael White, 'Russians ask Vietnam veterans to rehabilitate troops homeward bound from Afghanistan', *Guardian*, 24 August 1988, p. 1.
53. Alexander Kupriyanov, 'I tol'ko pyl' iz-pod sapog . . .', *Molodoi kommunist*, 1989, no. 6, p. 75.
54. Tsagolova, 'Snova snitsya voina'.

55. Ibid.
56. Kupriyanov, 'I tol'ko pyl'.
57. The US Department of Defense sponsored survey in 1971 showed that 50.9 per cent of US Army personnel in Vietnam had smoked marijuana, 28.5 per cent had used heroin and opium, and 30.8 per cent had taken other psychedelic drugs. See Alan H. Fisher, Jr., *Preliminary Findings from the 1971 DOD Survey of Drug Use* (Alexandria, Va.: Human Resources Research Organization, 1972) p. 23.
58. See Tsagolova, 'Snova snitsya voina'; Turshatov, 'How those returning . . .'; and Boris Kalachev, Oleg Osipenko, '"Molodo-zeleno" tsveta konopli . . .', *Molodoi kommunist*, 1988, no. 4, p. 57.
59. Turshatov, 'How those returning . . .'.
60. Tsagolova, 'Snova snitsya voina'.
61. Kalachev, Osipenko, '"Molodo-zeleno" tsveta konopli . . .'.
62. Sergei Biryukov, Oleg Minayev, Viktor Shaurin et al., 'Myi vmeste!', *Sobesednik*, January 1988, no. 3, p. 11.
63. Personal communication from Komsomol officials.
64. Igor Korolkov, 'Iz boya ne vyshli', *Sobesednik*, February 1987, no. 6, p. 5.
65. Igor Chernyak, 'Ne iskat' po zemle zhizni sladkoi', *Sobesednik*, December 1987, no. 49, p. 4.
66. Quoted in Podniecs et al., *Avrora*, p. 20.
67. Alexander Zver'ev, 'Opalennaya sovest'', *Sobesednik*, April 1987, no. 17, p. 15.
68. Ibid.
69. Korolkov, 'Iz boya'. See also Marat Serazhetdinov, 'Khochetsya v nebo', *Molodoi kommunist*, May 1987, no. 5, p. 68.
70. Korolkov, 'Iz boya'.
71. Such critics as Boris Kagarlitsky and Valeria Novodvorskaya were cited and taken to task by V. Gubenko and N. Piskarev, 'Samozvantsy i "Samodelshchiki"', *Komsomol'skaya pravda*, 31 January 1988, p. 2.
72. V. Kozin, 'Kaskad speshit na pomoshch'', *Komsomol'skaya pravda*, 20 January 1987, p. 2.
73. See Anatoly Yezhelev, *Izvestiya*, 1 August 1987, p. 3.
74. Yuri Shchekochikhin, 'O lyuberakh', i ne tol'ko o nikh', *Literaturnaya gazeta*, 11 March 1987, p. 1.
75. B. Vishnevsky, 'Koroli trubyat sbor', *Komsomol'skaya pravda*, 22 April 1987, p. 2.
76. Galina Nekrasova, 'Privet iz "Kalifornii"!', *Sobesednik*, February 1987, no. 11, p. 3.
77. Dina Gurevich, 'Nabolelo', *Smena*, October 1986, no. 20, p. 8.
78. Selikhov, 'Po trudnoi dorozhke'.
79. Vladimir Kolinichenko, 'Pochemu po komosomol'skuyu rabotu ne vydvigayut byvshikh voinov-internatsionalistov?', *Sobesednik*, May 1987, no. 22, p. 3.
80. Leonid Zhilnikov, 'Dlya nas net tyla', *Sobesednik*, March 1987, no. 5, p. 2.
81. Podniecs et al., *Avrora*, p. 25.

82. Dimitri Muratov, Yuri Sorokin, 'Duble vykhodit na svyaz', *Sobesednik*, March 1987, no. 13, pp. 8–9.
83. Laura Tsagolova, Igor Chernyak, 'Muzhskoi razgovor', *Sobesednik*, November 1987, no. 47, p. 2.
84. Gubenko, Piskarev, 'Samozvantsy . . .'.
85. Tsagolova, Chernyak, 'Muzhskoi razgovor'.
86. Chernyak, 'Ne iskat'', p. 5.
87. Ibid., p. 4.
88. Ibid., pp. 4–5.
89. V. Goncharenko, 'Budut plastinki', *Sobesednik*, November 1987, no. 47, p. 2.
90. Maggs, 'Legal rights', p. 3.

Index